Marcia L Watson

The Reliable Cook Book

Marcia L Watson

The Reliable Cook Book

ISBN/EAN: 9783744788670

Printed in Europe, USA, Canada, Australia, Japan

Cover: Foto ©Andreas Hilbeck / pixelio.de

More available books at **www.hansebooks.com**

THE

RELIABLE COOK BOOK.

Six Hundred Tested Recipes for Delicious and
Inexpensive Dishes for Breakfast,
Dinner and Supper.

COMPILED BY

MARCIA L. WATSON.

H. FRANKLIN JONES, Publisher,

669-671 Gates Avenue, Brooklyn, N. Y.

The Central Square Series.—Published Quarterly. By
Subscription—$1.00 per year—No. 83, July, 1898.—Entered
at the Brooklyn, N. Y., Post Office as second-class matter.

1

THE RELIABLE COOK BOOK.

PART I.

Brown Bread, Muffins, Gems, Rolls, etc.

Raised Sour Milk Bread.—Three cups of thick sour milk; dissolve one heaping teaspoonful soda in a little warm water, add a teaspoonful salt, and flour enough to mould like biscuit. Fill the pan two-thirds full. When fully risen bake about half an hour.

Butter-Milk Biscuit.—Add to one quart sifted flour, one teaspoonful soda, some salt and mix well. Then rub a tablespoonful of lard into the flour and pour in slowly two tea-cups moderately sour buttermilk. Do not make too stiff; bake in a quick oven.

Breakfast Cake.—Two eggs, two cups of sugar, two dessertspoonfuls of butter; beat well; add one cup of sweet milk, four teaspoonfuls cream tartar and two teaspoonfuls soda mixed with five cups of flour and a little salt.

Rye Muffins.—Two eggs, two cups milk, one-half cup molasses, four cups rye meal, one teaspoonful soda, salt.

Oatmeal Muffins.—One cup of oatmeal, one and one-half pints of flour, one teaspoonful salt, two of baking powder, one tablespoonful of lard, two eggs, one pint of milk. Sift together meal, flour, salt and baking powder; rub the lard in cold; and then add beaten eggs and milk.

Breakfast Gems.—One pint of sweet milk, one cup wheat flour, one cup graham flour, one egg, a little salt and sugar. Heat and grease tins before putting in the dough.

Buckwheat Pancakes.—For a family of four take one quart sour buttermilk, two-thirds teaspoon soda in buttermilk and beat well, a little salt, then stir in flour and not too stiff, and they will be splendid.

French Rolls.—Work one pound of butter into a pound of flour, put to it one beaten egg, two tablespoons of yeast, one teaspoon of salt and as much warm milk as will make a soft dough, strew flour over it, cover with a cloth and set in a warm place for an hour or more until light, flour your hands well, make in small rolls, bake in a quick oven.

Parker House Rolls.—Rub one tablespoon of lard into two quarts of flour. Scald one pint of milk; let it cool. Then add half a cup of yeast, and a very little sugar, and pour into the middle of the flour without stirring. Let it stand over night. In the morning knead well, and set in a warm place. Knead again, and roll out half an inch thick. Cut with biscuit cutter.

Muffins.—One quart of milk, two eggs, melt butter size of egg in the milk, one pound of flour and two teaspoonfuls of baking powder. Bake in gem irons in a hot oven.

Graham Bread.—Two and one-half cups of sour milk, four cups of graham flour, one-half cup of sugar, two tablespoonfuls of Orleans molasses, one teaspoon of soda, one teaspoon of salt, set in a warm place to rise three-fourths of an hour, then bake three-fourths of an hour. I hope some of the readers will try this and report.

Federal Bread.—To one pint of cream, or new milk warmed, add a large spoonful of good butter. Then take a large dining plate of sifted flour, and stir in with a knife. Add two eggs well beaten, a little salt, and two tablespoons of good yeast. Stir these well together, then put into the tins to rise. Do not disturb it after it has risen. Bake in the same tins three-fourths of an hour. When done cut off the top of each loaf. Spread thickly with butter, and serve immediately.

Corn Bread.—One large teacup Indian meal, one large teacup of flour, three eggs well beaten, one teaspoon of salt, one heaping tablespoon of butter melted but not hot, one heaping tablespoon of white sugar, one teaspoon of soda, two and one-half cups of milk, two teaspoons of cream tartar. Mix meal, flour, salt and cream tartar thoroughly. Stir the melted butter into the milk, also the sugar and soda. Add this mixture to the flour, meal, etc., then stir in the well-beaten eggs. Bake in a deep pan nearly an hour.

Brown Bread.—One cup of white meal, one cup of rye, one cup of flour, one of molasses, two teaspoons soda, one teaspoon salt, mix with cold water, quite thin. Steam three hours.

Steamed Indian Loaf.—One cup flour, two cups corn meal, three-fourths cup molasses or brown sugar, one pint of milk, sour or sweet, a little salt, one-half teaspoonful soda; takes two hours to steam.

Brown Bread.—One and one-half cups of graham, two cups of corn meal, one cup of molasses, one teaspoonful each of salt and saleratus, add enough sour milk to mix stiffly, put in a covered pail and set in a kettle of boiling water and let it boil one and one-half hours.

Corn Bread.—Three cups sour milk, one cup of flour, one-half cup sugar, one scant teaspoonful of soda, a little salt, and corn meal enough to make a batter.

Brown Bread.—Four cups sifted Indian meal, two cups flour, one cup molasses, one teaspoon soda, salt, sweet milk enough to make a thin batter. Steam three hours, then set in the oven to dry.

Milk Yeast Bread.—Take one pint of wheat flour or middlings, stir into it one tablespoonful of sugar, salt and ginger, and one teaspoonful of saleratus, mix well and sift, then put this dry mixture in a glass jar and keep air tight. The day before you want to bake, take two tablespoonfuls of this mixture and pour on three-fourths of a cup of boiling water, stir well, then set in a warm place until the next morning, then take one pint of new milk and same of boiling water, and a half teaspoon of salt, add the yeast and stir in flour until quite thick, then keep this quite warm and in a few hours it will be a light foam, then dissolve one half teaspoonful saleratus in a little hot water and stir it into the sponge, stir in more flour and mould into loaves as soft as can be handled and rise again and bake.

Graham Bread.—One gill of yeast, one gill molasses, three quarts graham flour, one teaspoon soda, pinch of salt, one quart of warm water; stir together and let rise, then steam two hours and bake in a moderate oven thirty minutes.

Brown Bread (Raised).—One pint of Indian meal scalded in one pint of water, one pint of wheat meal, one-half cup of molasses, one-half teaspoonful of soda dissolved in it, one-half cup of yeast, a little salt. When risen, steam three hours.

Brown Bread.—Four large cups sweet skimmed milk (scalding improves it), one cup sour milk, one teaspoonful soda, one teaspoonful salt, equal quantities Indian and rye meal; bake one hour and a-half in a stove oven, then steam two hours.

Cinnamon Rolls.—Make a biscuit dough of one pint of flour, one and a-half teaspoonfuls of baking powder, half a teaspoonful of salt, and a full tablespoonful each of butter and lard. Rub the shortening into the flour, having first thoroughly mixed in the salt and baking powder. Use enough new milk to make into a soft dough. Roll it out very thin and sprinkle on a cup of coffee crushed sugar, well mixed with a small teaspoonful of cinnamon. Then roll it up tightly, and cut across in slices from three-quarters to an inch thick. Lay them upon a biscuit pan and bake quickly.

Noodles.—Mix a very stiff dough out of three eggs, a little salt and flour, roll into very thin sheets, allow to lay a few moments, then roll all up together and cut into shreds with a sharp knife, shake apart and allow to dry, (one can dry thoroughly, put away in a paper poke and use at any time). These can then be added to beef broth, chicken soup or may be cooked about fifteen minutes in salt water, dipped from the water and browned, butter poured over for seasoning, or they are very good seasoned with plenty of milk, butter and cream with a little thickening.

French Toast.—Take three eggs, beat well, and add one-teacupful milk, dip the slices of bread in this batter and fry in butter till a good brown, eat while hot.

Nice Light Dumplings.—One cup flour, one tablespoon baking powder, a little salt, mix this well with the flour and then add sweet milk enough to make a stiff batter; drop in small spoonfuls into boiling soup and boil twenty minutes.

Cold Short-Cake.—Make a nice short-cake, and after it is cool or cold, split and spread with butter, then spread thickly with fruit, if peaches cut them up in rather small pieces and sprinkle plenty of sugar over them, then spread the fruit thickly with whipped cream. The two layers of short-cake can be used separately or piled one over the other as desired. This way of preparing short-cake is considered more digestible than to be eaten warm. Of course any fruit can be used.

Best Oatmeal Gems.—One cup raw oatmeal soaked over night in two cups sour milk. In the morning add two eggs, sufficient soda, a little salt, and enough graham flour to make a pretty stiff batter. Have gem pans on the stove, and when filled bake in a very hot oven about fifteen minutes.

Delicate Breakfast Rolls.—Take one quart sifted flour, two teaspoonfuls Horsford's baking powder, one teaspoonful salt, three and a-half gills sweet milk and water, or milk alone; drop with a spoon into the "Gem" baking pan. Before mixing the above, set the "Gem" pan on the stove, and let it get very hot before filling, so that the rolls will begin to bake as soon as they touch the pan.

Corn Cake.—One cup of corn meal, one cup of milk, one-fourth cup of sugar, two eggs, one and one-fourth cup of flour, one teaspoonful of soda, and two of cream of tartar, three table-spoonfuls of melted butter. Beat up the eggs and sugar, dissolve the soda in the milk and add it, then stir in the corn meal. Mix the cream of tartar and flour together, and add. Put in the melted butter last. Bake in a flat pan.

Buckwheat Johnny Cake.—Take one pint buttermilk, or sour milk, break in an egg, add a little salt, but not thicken to a stiff batter, put in a large spoonful of melted lard or butter, and last thing put in half teaspoon soda, or more according to sourness of milk. This is very nice for breakfast or tea, with maple syrup.

Breakfast Cakes.—One cup sour milk, one cup sour cream, one-half cup sugar, two small teaspoonsful soda, one-half cup currants, well washed, a little salt, flour enough to roll thin. Cut with the biscuit-cutter, and bake in a quick oven. To be eaten cold.

English Muffins.—Take yeast-bread dough that has risen over night, roll into thin, round cakes, as large as a small breakfast plate. Bake on a hot griddle, turning them over once. When done split them open and butter.

Cakes for Breakfast.—One cup of Indian meal, one tea-spoonful of salt, one tablespoon of sugar, scald the meal, then add two tablespoonfuls of milk or water, one egg, and one table-spoonful of flour, stir well, butter your griddle, put on large spoonfuls of the batter and fry a light brown.

Graham Gems.—Two cups graham, one cup milk, one-half cup sugar, one egg, two teaspoons Congress yeast powder or any other baking powder. Have gem pans heating while mixing above.

Sour Cream Biscuit.—One pint sour cream, one teaspoon soda, one of salt, flour to make a soft dough. Roll to half inch thick, put in a pan not allowing to touch each other. Bake them in three minutes' oven. Try them, they are delicious.

Sugar Biscuits.—Three eggs, two cups sugar, one sour cream, half pound butter, half teaspoon soda, one teaspoon cream tartar, nutmeg. Bake as soft as you can handle.

Sour Cream Biscuit.—One teacup sour cream, one-half teacup buttermilk mixed together, one teaspoon saleratus dissolv-ed in a teaspoon of hot water and beaten into the cream, one-half teaspoonful of salt, flour enough to knead soft. Bake quickly. This will make twelve biscuits.

Flannel Cakes.—Cut dry, light bread in pieces, put over it enough sour milk to cover, let it stand over night, in the morn-ing wash it well, and to every quart of bread add one egg well beaten, a teaspoonful of soda, a pinch of salt and flour to make a moderately thin batter ; bake on a griddle.

Rice Muffins.—Two cups of milk, one cup of boiled rice, one-quarter cup of sugar, one-half cup of yeast, a small piece of butter, flour to make stiff batter. Rise over night. In the morn-ing drop into muffin rings without stirring.

Rye Gems.—One egg, one cup sweet milk, one-fourth cup of sugar, one heaping teaspoon cream tartar, one-half teaspoon soda, one cup flour, one cup rye meal.

Graham Gems.—Three eggs, three cups of milk, three cups of graham flour, and some salt. Beat thoroughly.

Parker Rolls.—One quart of new milk, scalded, one cup of sugar, stirred in while hot, when cool stir in one-half cup of yeast, make a hole in a pan of flour, put in two tablespoons of lard, one-half teaspoon of saleratus and a little salt, then pour in the milk and let it rise without stirring. When light make into dough and let rise again, then work well and roll out thin and spread with butter ; cut out with cake cutter and lap together and rise and bake.

Potato Biscuits.—Two cups of mashed potato, one teaspoon of salt, one half pint of warm water, one quart of flour, a small piece of lard, one cup of yeast ; knead all together and let rise over night. In the morning roll out and cut same as biscuits, rise and bake for breakfast.

Mush Biscuit—One and one-half cups of (corn) mush, one cup of yeast, a little salt, flour to knead thoroughly. Let rise over night, in the morning make into biscuits for breakfast.

Waffles.—One quart of sour cream, four eggs, one-half tea-spoonful of soda and flour enough to be as thick as batter cakes. Sour milk can be used if cream is scarce by putting in a piece of butter the size of an egg.

Fried Cakes.—Two-thirds cup sugar, one-half cup butter milk, three tablespoons lard, one egg, one-half teaspoonful soda. Mix soft.

Sally Lunn.—One quart flour, two eggs, one pint milk, two tablespoons of sugar, piece of butter size of two large sized eggs, one-half teaspoonful salt, two teaspoons cream of tartar, one teaspoon of soda. Beat butter and sugar together. Add eggs, well beaten. Mix the soda with the milk, and the cream of tartar with the flour.

Nice Corn Cake.—One cup of flour, one-half cup of corn meal, one cup of sour milk, one-half teaspoon of soda, one table-spoon of sugar, a little melted butter, and a very little salt. Bake in a quick oven.

Breakfast Gems.—Two cups of rolled oats soaked over night in one and a-half cups of sour milk, then add a-half cup of molasses, one cup wheat flour, one teaspoon of soda, one of salt, two eggs. Mix thoroughly and bake quick.

A Good Breakfast Dish.—Toast slices of bread, as many as you need. For two persons take two eggs, a good half cup of

milk, butter half as big as an egg, salt to taste ; let the milk come
to a boil, beat the eggs in and cook until it thickens ; butter the
bread, turn the egg upon it while hot.

Flour Gems.—One egg, tablespoonful of sugar, two of butter, one and a-half cups of sweet milk, two and one-half cups of
flour, three teaspoonfuls of baking powder, beat well. Have the
gem tins buttered and hot, put in and bake quick.

Spanish Buns.—One pint sugar, one cup milk, one pint
flour, one pint butter, four eggs, one tablespoonful cloves and one
of cinnamon, three teaspoons baking powder. Bake in square
tins and ice thinly.

Muffins.—Beat two eggs into a quart of buttermilk, stir in
flour to make a thick batter, one teaspoonful salt, and the same
of soda, bake in a hot oven in well-greased tins. Muffins of all
kinds should only be cut just around the edge, then pulled apart
with the fingers.

Sally Lunn.—One cup each of milk and sugar, two eggs,
tablespoon butter, two teaspoons cream tartar, one of soda (or
two heaping teaspoons baking powder instead of cream tartar and
soda), flour for thick batter. Bake quickly.

Virginia Muffins.—One and one-half cups of milk, one-half
cup of sugar, one egg, three cups of flour, two teaspoonfuls of
baking powder, butter the size of a hen's egg ; beat until very
light and bake in a quick oven.

Mrs. Brooks' Nice Rye Biscuit.—Take a cupful of molasses, and a cupful and a half of milk, a teaspoonful of soda,
stir about as stiff as gingerbread, with rye-meal three parts and
flour a fourth part. Bake in hot gem pans and serve with butter
for breakfast.

Best Johnny Cake.—One cup sour milk, one cup sweet,
one good egg well beaten, three cups Indian, one cup wheat,
half cup molasses, add thereto, half cup of sugar with one spoon
of butter, now, salt and soda each a spoon, mix up quickly and
bake it soon.

Buttermilk Muffins.—Beat well two eggs, into one pint
and three gills of buttermilk, stir in flour to make a thick batter,

add a teaspoonful of salt, and the same of soda, bake in a hot oven, in well greased tins. Nice for breakfast.

Drop Biscuits.—For a family of three, take two cups flour, two large teaspoonfuls baking powder, small pinch salt. Sift all together and stir in as much sweet milk, cream and all, as will make it as stiff as can be stirred. Drop on greased tins and bake in a quick oven.

Fried Cakes—One cup sour milk, three big spoons cream or lard, three teaspoons cloves, one and one-half teaspoons ginger, one teaspoon soda, flour enough to make a soft paste and fry in hot lard.

Corn Muffins.—Three cups of corn meal, one-half cup of sifted wheat flour, three eggs well beaten, two tablespoons of butter, one teaspoon of soda, dissolved in one pint of buttermilk, and a little salt. Beat them well together, pour into rings, and bake a nice brown in the oven.

PART II.

Meats, Fowl, Soups, Etc.

Chicken Pie.—Two young chickens boiled tender, line the sides of baking dish with puff paste, put a layer of chicken, place strips of pastry over with lumps of fresh butter, pepper and salt sprinkled over, then cover the top with rich puff paste, bake in slow oven, don't let it get dry, keep juicy with soup from chicken.

Southern Chicken Pie.—Boil a chicken until it is tender, then take a deep earthen dish and put into it a layer of the chicken, well seasoned with butter, pepper and salt, then put a layer of cold boiled rice on this, and so on until you have exhausted your resources, taking care to have a layer of rice on top. Put this into the oven and let it remain there until it is very hot and then serve.

Chicken Pie.—Crust, one quart of flour, three heaping teaspoons of baking powder, one small teaspoon of salt. Mix these well together with the hand. Rub into this mixture one tablespoon of butter, and one tablespoon of lard. When thoroughly mixed, add just enough milk to make a soft dough. Stir with hand quickly, without much kneading. Then roll out about three-fourths of an inch thick. Inside, take a chicken. Clean and cut up. Cut thin slices of salt fat pork. Put a thick layer of pork slices in the bottom of a stew pan. On these lay the fowl. Add a very little salt and pepper. Just cover the chicken with water and close the pan tightly. Let it stew very slowly for half an hour. Then take out the pieces of chicken and place into a pie dish. Take some of the gravy and stir in a large spoonful of flour. Season, and pour over the chicken. Cut a piece of butter in thin slices and lay on top of the fowl. Cover with the crust. Bake half an hour and serve hot.

Chicken Stew.—Cut up two fowls, fry out three slices of pork, add a small onion, sliced, and cook until done. Lay in the chicken, and season each layer with salt and a little pepper, cover with water. When nearly tender add five or six potatoes, sliced. Cover with dumplings. When the chicken is taken up, there should be just liquid enough left to thicken for a gravy.

Fricasseed Chicken.—Put the chicken, cut up, into a saucepan with barely enough water to cover it, and stew gently till tender. Have a frying pan with a few slices of salt pork in it; drain the chicken and fry with the pork until of a rich brown; then remove from the pan, and put in the broth in which the chicken was stewed; thicken with browned flour mixed smooth in a little water, and season with pepper. Put the chicken and pork back into the gravy, let it simmer a few minutes and serve hot.

Chicken Pie.—Boil chickens in water, barely to cover them, forty minutes. Skim the water carefully. Take them out in a dish, and cut them up as they should be carved if placed upon the table. If the skin is very thick, remove it. Have ready, lined with a thick paste, a deep dish of a size proportionate to the number of chickens you wish to use; put in the pieces, with the hearts and livers, in layers; sprinkle each layer with flour, salt and pepper, and put on each piece of chicken a thin layer of butter; do this until you have laid in all the pieces; put rather more of the spice, flour and butter over the top layer than on the previous ones, and pour in as much of the liquor in which the chickens were boiled as you can without danger of its boiling over. Lay on the upper crust, and close the edges very carefully with flour and water; prick the top with a knife; cut leaves of crust and ornament it. Bake two hours. The crust for chicken pie should be twice as thick as for fruit pies. Use mace and nutmeg if you wish.

Chicken Salad.—Take the chicken off of the bones. Cut it into dice like pieces. Wash a head of celery, and, also, cut into dice like pieces. Mix with the chicken. Pour over it Mayonnaise dressing. Garnish with olives and cold boiled eggs, and serve.

Salmi of Duck.—Cut up cold duck, as for fricassee. Put it in a pan with one ounce of butter. Fry brown quickly. When done add a pint of onions. Just cover with boiling water. Season with salt and pepper. Take some stale bread. Cut in heart shaped pieces. Brown them in a quick oven. When the salmi is done, pour it upon a hot dish.   Garnish it with the bread, and serve.

Broiled Bacon.—Dip slices of thin bacon in bread crumbs, fry on a hot gridiron, turn when done.   Serve with gravy made of sweet cream, parsley, season with pepper and salt.

Fried Apples and Bacon.—Core and slice round, without paring, some tart, well-flavored apples.   Cut into thin slices some middlings of excellent bacon or pork, and fry in their own fat almost to crispness.   Take out the meat and keep hot while you fry the apples in the fat left in the pan ; add a little sugar to taste. Drain, and lay upon the slices of meat.

Cold Beef.—One cup of cold beef, chopped fine, one egg, one-third cup bread crumbs ; season with pepper, salt and sage and make into balls and fry in butter or lard.

Beef Cakes.—Chop up some beef that is partly cooked with a little smoked pork fat and season with salt, pepper and onions; mix well and form into small cakes.   Fry them light brown and serve with a good gravy made of soup stock thickened with brown flour.

Beef Fritters.—Good for breakfast.   Chop pieces of steak or cold roast beef very fine.   Make a batter of milk, flour and an egg, and mix the meat with it.   Season with pepper, salt and a little parsley.   Put a lump of butter into a saucepan, let it melt, then drop the batter into it from a large spoon.   Fry until brown.

Cold Beef.—Mince it fine, with pepper, salt and onions, some rich gravy, and put it into tins three parts full, fill them up with mashed potatoes and brown in oven.

A Breakfast Dish.—Take cold beef, pork or veal, the more variety the better, and hash it fine, mix with two eggs, and a little grated onion (or not as preferred), a little melted butter, two pounded crackers and pepper and salt to taste; roll in balls, and fry in butter flavored with lemon juice.

Breakfast Dish No. 2.—Take some cold boiled or baked meat, chop it fine, then put in about the same amount of tomatoes, either canned or fresh, and chop them fine and mix well together.   Put a layer of bread crumbs in a buttered pan, put the meat and tomatoes in, seasoned with salt and pepper, then another layer of bread crumbs. Pour a cup of water, or the water in which meat has been boiled is better, over the top and bake one hour in a moderate oven.

Ham Balls.—Take two well-beaten eggs and half a cup of bread crumbs, mix well together and add some fine chopped ham. Make into cakes and fry in hot fat.

Rissoles.—To make rissoles take any kind of nice cold roast meat, chop it fine, salt and spice it to taste. Roll a tablespoonful in very thin pastry crust, and fry quickly in butter or lard.

Spiced Beef.—Five pounds of the shank boiled five hours with celery seed. Drain off the gelatine and then chop the meat very fine, and pepper and salt to taste, and put it into a cloth on a platter. Cover with a cloth and press.

Spiced Beef.—Boil a piece of beef in a quart of water until very tender, take from the water, chop fine, season with salt, pepper, a half teaspoonful of cloves; add water in which the meat was boiled, place in a mould, place weight on and press. When well pressed together, cut it into slices. Any piece of beef will answer for spiced beef, unless too fat.

Beef Shank.—Boil till the meat will slip off the bones readily, take out bones, chop up meat and season to taste; we generally only use salt and pepper; put back the liquid in which it was boiled, let it boil, and then turn out in a deep dish to cool; when cold slice and serve.

Beef Tea.—Chop a piece of lean beef, put in an earthern jar, cover close and set in a kettle of water; boil four or five hours, or until juice is all extracted; salt and strain.

Stewed Beef with Onions.—Cover the bottom of a frying pan with thinly shaved slices of fat pork. When the fat is all tried out, lay in a thick steak cut from the round, and let it brown upon both sides; then take it off and add one tablespoonful of flour to the pork; stir it till it is smooth, then put in a pint of water, a tablespoonful of catsup, a teaspoonful of currant jelly and a large onion, chopped fine. Add salt and pepper to the taste, and put the steak back in the gravy to boil slowly for two hours and a-half, covering closely and adding more water from the teakettle if necessary. When done lay the steak upon a dish, put a piece of butter upon it, and pour the gravy over.

Roast of Calf's Liver.—Wash thoroughly and wipe dry; cut a long, deep hole in the side, stuff with crumbs, onion and bacon, chopped; salt and pepper to taste, a bit of butter and one egg; sew or tie together the liver, lard it over and bake in the oven, basting often; serve with gravy and currant jelly.

Dried Beef in Cream.—Shave the beef very fine, pour over it boiling water and let stand a little while. Pour off the water and pour off good rich cream and let come to a boil. If you have not cream use milk and butter thickened with a little flour, season with pepper and serve on toast.

Fresh Pork and Potatoes.—Take a roast of pork, sprinkle it with sage and salt, and put into the oven to roast. Two hours before dinner have prepared enough potatoes for the family; put them in the dripping-pan under the pork; when done they should be nicely browned.

Mock Duck.—Take some round steak, make a stuffing as for turkey, spread over the steak, roll it up and tie it, roast about three-quarters of an hour.

Veal Pie.—Stew small pieces of veal until tender ; season with butter, pepper and salt. Thicken the broth (of which have plenty), with batter made of milk, flour and a well-beaten egg. Pour into a deep pan and cover with a rich biscuit dough, bake until a nice brown.

Rabbit Pie.—Cut up, soak in salt water half an hour, and boil nearly tender. Cut some fat pork in strips, and boil two eggs hard ; put in the pie dish, lined with paste, a layer of the pork, then rabbit, slices of egg, salt, pepper, butter, mace, and lemon juice ; thicken with flour the water the rabbit was boiled in, pour over, cover with paper, and bake one hour.

Beefsteak and Onions.—Cut up six onions very fine ; put them in a saucepan with two cupfuls of hot water, about two ounces of good butter, some pepper and salt ; dredge in flour. Stew until the onions are quite soft ; then have the steak broiled; put into the saucepan with the onions ; simmer about ten minutes and send to the table very hot.

Stuffed Beefsteak.—Take a rump steak about an inch thick, make a stuffing the usual way, spread over the steak, roll up and tie securely, put in an iron kettle with not too much water and stew slowly about two hours, when done thicken the gravy and pour over, carve in slices through the steak and stuffing.

Hamburg Steak with Onions.—Take of the upper cut of a round of beef one and one-half pounds. Add to it a small bit of fat. Have the butcher chop it fine. Form it with the hands into a flat oval shape about an inch thick. Place it carefully on the broiler (do not break it), and broil just as you would a steak, turning often. It is much nicer if left a little rare. When done remove to the platter and pour over two tablespoonfuls of melted butter, a little salt and pepper, and the onions previously cooked. Clean six onions. Chop fine. Put a tablespoonful of suet in an iron spider ; one teaspoonful of sugar and the chopped onions, with a little salt and pepper. Cook one-half hour or until tender, turning occasionally. Keep them closely covered. When done pour over the steak.

Hamburg Steak.—Chop one pound of round steak fine, season with a tablespoonful of onion juice, a little black pepper and half a teaspoonful of salt ; mix well, form in small, flat cakes and fry in hot lard. Make gravy and pour over.

Rolled Beefsteak.—Take two pounds of round steak, cut in a thick slice. Make a stuffing of a cup of bread crumbs and a teaspoonful of melted butter. Season with sage, salt and pepper. Lay the steak on a board, trim off the fat and hack one side of it thoroughly with a knife. Do not cut through the steak. Spread the stuffing on the chopped side, roll the meat over and fasten with wooden toothpicks to keep it. Put over it a few thin slices of salt pork. Then tie all up nicely with twine. Lay in a saucepan with a pint of water and a piece of carrot and onion cut fine, a saltspoonful of salt and a teaspoonful of vinegar. Let this simmer for three hours ; then take it up, remove the string and toothpicks, sprinkle flour over it and set in the oven to brown. Skim gravy, and when meat is browned pour over it and serve. This is very nice when well cooked. The success of the dish depends on simmering slowly and browning quickly.

Steak Rolled and Baked—Dust a little pepper and salt over a nice steak cut not more than half an inch thick. Prepare a forcemeat by mixing a quarter pound of sifted bread crumbs with two dessertspoonfuls finely chopped suet, one dessertspoonful chopped parsley and a small piece of lemon peel shred very fine. Season with salt and pepper, and bind the mixture with a well beaten egg. Place this forcemeat on one end of the steak, roll up tightly as possible, bind securely with twine, ends and all, to prevent the escape of the forcemeat. Wrap the rolled steak in a well-greased paper and lay it in a dripping pan in which is two ounces of hot dripping. Bake in a hot oven, basting frequently. Allow twenty minutes for each pound of steak. Ten minutes before taking from the oven remove the paper to let the outside brown. Serve with hot boiled potatoes and brown gravy.

Pea Soup.—Use one pint of dried peas for every four quarts of soup. Wash the peas well, then put them in six quarts of cold water. Let them come slowly to a boil. Add some kind of a meat bone, with a carrot and an onion. Simmer for three hours. Strain through a sieve. Place on the fire again, and put in one tablespoon of flour, and the same of butter, mix together. Cut some bread into dice-like pieces, and brown in the oven. Place them in the bottom of a tureen, and pour the soup over them.

Pea Soup.—Take one-third of a pound of split peas. Put into three pints of water. Cut the pork into pieces the size of dice, with one onion, one-half bunch of parsley chopped fine. Boil all two hours. Add water, so that when done there will be three pints.

Tomato Soup. (Equal to oyster).—Cook till done one quart of tomatoes, add first one teaspoon saleratus, then pepper freely, half cup butter, then add two quarts new milk, let boil till it boils to the top of kettle, then set off and add salt to taste.

Tomato Soup.—Take one-half can tomatoes, stew and strain through a sieve ; season to taste with pepper, salt, a little sugar and butter

Tomato Soup.—One quart tomatoes, one small onion cut fine, one quart water, one level tablespoon of salt, black pepper or red pepper. Boil forty-five minutes. Sift it. When it comes to boiling again put in three tablespoons of browned flour stirred with a little cold milk, a pinch of soda and a pint of milk and let it boil twenty minutes. Butter the size of an egg.

Tomato Soup.—One quart of tomatoes, two heaping table-spoons flour, one tablespoon butter, one teaspoon sugar (some use twice as much), one teaspoon salt, one pint hot water. Let the tomatoes and water come to a boil ; rub the flour, butter and one spoonful of the tomatoes together, and stir into the boiling mixture. Season to taste, and boil fifteen minutes longer. Rub through a sieve, and serve with a piece of butter and nicely-toasted bread. Extra nice.

Green Corn Soup is one of the most delicious of vegetable soups for Summer. Scrape or cut the thinnest possible shaving from each row of corn on the cob, and with the back of a knife press out the pulp, leaving the hull on the cob. There should be about a pint of this pulp. Break the cobs and put on to boil in enough cold water to cover them, boil thirty minutes and strain. There should be about a pint of this corn water, and when it boils again add the corn pulp, and cook fifteen minutes. Add salt, pepper, a half teaspoonful sugar, and a pint of boiling milk or cream. Thicken with a teaspoonful of flour cooked in a table-spoonful of butter. Boil a minute or two and serve at once.

Spinach Soup.—Wash and trim one quart of spinach and put into a saucepan holding three quarts of boiling water and three tablespoonfuls of salt. Boil rapidly with the cover off till tender, which will be in about eight minutes. Next drain through a colander, run plenty of cold water on it, chop fine and rub through a sieve with a wooden spoon. While the spinach is boiling prepare the soup as follows : Put the milk over the fire to boil, first putting into the saucepan two gills of cold water to prevent burning. Mix together over the fire one ounce of butter, the same of flour, till they bubble ; then slowly add the boiling milk, season with salt to taste, half a saltspoonful of white pepper, one-quarter of a saltspoonful of grated nutmeg, stir in enough spinach to color a light green and serve hot.

Lobster Stew.—Select two medium sized lobsters, pick out all the meat, also all the inside dressing and chop all together; have milk, butter, pepper and salt all hot and add the lobster with one small tablespoon of sugar, let boil up once and serve with oyster crackers, just the same as oyster stew.

Julienne Soup.—Make a stock as for clear soup. Finely shred half an ounce of onion, quarter of an ounce of celery leaves, and three ounces each of cabbage, string-beans, carrot, and white and yellow turnips. Gently simmer all together till the vegetables are tender. Season. Chop up the yolk of a hard boiled egg, and put in just before serving.

Calf's Head Soup.—Put the head on in water enough to cover it entirely, and let it boil until the bones will slip out. Then take it out on a dish, throw the bones back into the pot, lay the brains on a plate, chop the head and tongue quite fine and season highly with pepper, salt and onions. Then take the bones out again, put back the meat and throw in a dozen grains of allspice. Take the brains, with a small portion of the tongue chopped very fine; season with salt, pepper and parsley and add stale bread crumbs sufficient to make into balls the size of a walnut. Then beat well the yolk of an egg, roll the balls in it, dust them with flour, fry them a nice brown and put them in the soup dish before putting in the soup. This soup is greatly improved by adding a gill of wine, one of mushroom and one of walnut catsup, just before serving. Thicken with browned flour.

Rivel Soup.—Allow a quart or more sweet milk to come to a boil. Rub an egg into about a pint of flour till it is in fine crumbs, then stir slowly into boiling milk, add salt, and serve immediately.

Vermicelli Soup.—Blanch the vermicelli by putting the paste into plenty of boiling water, with one tablespoon of salt to each quart of water. Boil until tender. Drain it, and put into cold water until wanted. To every quart of stock add one ounce of vermicelli. Put into the hot soup long enough to heat thoroughly, before serving. Season.

Mock Turtle Soup.—Take a calf's head which has been thoroughly cleaned. Remove brains and boil separately. Put the head in a pot with more water than will cover it. Let it boil for an hour and skim frequently. Take it out and when cool cut the meat into pieces about an inch square. Scrape and cut the tongue in the same manner. Lay all these pieces aside, then put into the water in which the head was boiled about three pounds of leg of beef and a knuckle of veal, the meat cut small and the bones broken. Add four or five onions, a small bunch of herbs, a carrot and turnip sliced and some whole black pepper. Boil slowly four or five hours, take off, cool, and strain, remove all fat. Put a good sized lump of butter in a stew pan, add two handfuls of flour, let it brown, stirring all the time. Add a little of the soup, a sprig or two of parsley and boil fifteen minutes, strain and add to the rest of the soup, with the brains pounded, and boil for thirty minutes. Add a glass of sherry, if liked, and when in tureen put in some force meat balls.

Celery Soup.—One pint of milk and a little over a pint of boiling water; rub together one tablespoonful of butter and two of flour; stir into boiling milk until smooth; add one teaspoonful of salt and one of celery extract; use one-half a bunch of celery, boiled (leaves and all) in the water given in the recipe; boil one hour.

Bean Soup.—One pint of soup beans, one medium sized onion, one large tablespoonful of butter, salt and pepper to suit the taste. Pick over the beans, wash clean, and soak over night; in the morning drain off the water and put them in a kettle with two quarts of cold water. Let them boil slowly until they are tender; slice the onion very thin and add to the soup with the butter, pepper and salt. When the onion is tender, pass the soup through a coarse sieve, and serve very hot. A few hard boiled eggs sliced in the soup just before serving is an improvement.

Potato Soup.—For this use three potatoes boiled soft in salted water or a pint (two cupfuls) of mashed potato left from dinner. Cook a small onion and a stalk of celery with a pint of milk in a double boiler, add to the potatoes with salt and pepper, celery salt and a pinch of cayenne pepper, rub through the strainer and put on to boil. Thicken with half a tablespoonful of butter, and let it boil five minutes, adding more hot milk if too thick, and serving very hot. An ornamental effect and an agreeable flavor to many is gained by adding a tablespoonful of finely chopped parsley just before serving.

Potato Soup.—Wash and pare three potatoes and let them soak in cold water for half an hour. Put them into boiling water and cook very soft. Put a pint of milk on to boil in the double boiler with a teaspoonful of chopped onion and a stalk of celery. When the potatoes are done drain and mash them. Add the boiling milk and season with one teaspoonful of salt and a little pepper. Rub through a strainer, and put on to boil again. Melt a teaspoonful of butter in a small dish. Stir into it one half tablespoonful of flour, and when well mixed stir into the boiling soup. Let boil five minutes and serve very hot.

Brunoise Soup.—Put one quart of soup meat over the fire in two quarts of cold water, and bring it slowly to a boil. Skim it clear. Peel a carrot, onion and leek, cut in dice, and with a little celery, put over the fire to brown with an ounce of butter, a teaspoon of powdered sugar, and a quarter of a saltspoon of pepper. Take the meat from the soup; put it with the vegetables; strain the broth into them. Season with salt. Simmer till meat and vegetables are tender. Take out the meat. Serve hot.

Clam Chowder.—Brown some pork scraps and three onions together until a light brown. Into a large pot put a large layer of sliced potato, then a layer of soft clams, sprinkling a little salt, pepper, mace, cloves and allspice; then another layer of potatoes, clams and seasoning. When boiled put on the back part of the stove and let simmer ten minutes. Before serving add a quart of milk. Let it all boil. Then put in the pork scraps and onions and half a tumbler of sherry wine.

PART III.

Fish and Oysters.

Salmon Salad No. 1.—Take one can salmon and the white part of a large bunch of celery, chop fine and mix with mayonnaise dressing.

Salmon Salad No. 2.—Yolks of three eggs, half cup cream, half cup vinegar, two teaspoonfuls brown sugar, salt, pepper and celery seed to taste; let this mixture boil thick like custard, and pour over one can of salmon. This dressing makes a splendid potato salad.

Scalloped Lobster.—Line a baking dish with small pieces of butter, put in a layer of lobster picked in small pieces. Sprinkle over a little salt, pepper, lemon juice and a layer of bread crumbs, repeat having the crumbs on top. Pour over two cups of milk and bake half an hour. Serve hot.

Scalloped Salmon.—Take two cups of milk and when boiling thicken with a tablespoonful of cornstarch, wet with cold milk ; this is for the sauce. Then lay in an earthen dish a layer of salmon, sprinkled with salt and pepper; then a layer of cracker or bread crumbs, moisten with the sauce, and so on in this way fill up the dish, having the last layer of bread crumbs. Put bits of butter over the top in a hot oven and bake about twenty minutes. Serve hot. This makes a very nice dish to get up in a hurry for unexpected company on a day when the larder is lean. Canned salmon is as good for the purpose as fresh.

Baked Halibut.—Have it sliced as for frying ; lay one slice in baking pan with a few bits of salt pork (a very few) beneath it to keep it from sticking. On this put a bit or two of sweet butter and such seasoning as you like ; be wary of overdoing it ; on this place a second piece, treating it the same and continue to lay the fish in piles of three slices until all are prepared. Moisten occasionally with water until nearly done, then pour over it a cup of sweet cream or new milk and serve with egg sauce or mock cream for gravy. A nice egg sauce is made by taking one pint of milk, beating in one tablespoonful of farina or cornstarch or common flour, first evenly moistened in a little milk ; add two well-beaten eggs and boil five minutes and pour over the fish as it lies on the fish-platter or serve apart as you choose.

Boiled Salmon with Sauce.—Slice one onion in boiling water, add a little salt, put in three pounds of salmon, with whole cloves, allspice, pepper and let them simmer for three quarters of an hour ; keep well covered. When done take up with great care on a platter ; let drain well. For sauce, put butter size of an egg in a frying pan with one tablespoonful of flour ; when light brown add part of the water the fish has been boiled in until it forms a nice gravy ; this should boil up in a few minutes, then remove from the fire ; stir in briskly a well-beaten egg, pour the gravy over the fish ; set away to cool. This dish should be eaten cold. A little cream added to the gravy gives it a nice flavor.

To Fry Small Fish.—Make two or three deep gashes in the fish on each side, and rub salt and pepper over them, even into the cuts you have made. Roll in flour or Indian meal, and fry in butter or salt pork, tried out. As soon as the fish cleaves from the bone, remove to a hot platter, as too much cooking is as bad as too little, and this rule is a sure test of the correct cooking of fish. A tablespoonful of fat is enough to use, and will brown a spider full of fish well, although from time to time little pieces of butter may need to be added to prevent burning.

Baked Fish.—Dress your fish nicely, salt to taste, and lay it out flat in your nicely greased dripping-pan, leaving the flesh side up. Scatter small pieces of butter on the fish, and then bake until done—from twenty minutes to half an hour, according to the size of fish. Then pour over the fish a teacupful of sweet cream, and return to the oven until nicely browned. A very hot oven is required to cook fish in this way.

Salt Codfish.—Pare your potatoes, and lay the codfish, nicely skinned, on top of them. Boil and serve with a simple gravy of flour and water well cooked, seasoned and heavily buttered. For breakfast " pick up " finely what is left, and, in the morning, heat over in just water enough to moisten it, butter and pepper it well, and spread like sandwiches on thin slices of bread made into egg-toast. Moisten your slices of bread in cold water, then dip in beaten egg and milk and lay on a nicely-buttered frying-pan over a quick fire; turn bread quickly, spread on your fish and serve hot.

Baked Bass.—Wash well a fresh bass. Wipe dry. Stuff it with stuffing as for roast turkey. Then lay it in a dripping-pan. Cover the fish with slices of pork; season with salt and pepper. Bake in a moderate oven a little over half an hour. Baste occasionally with a little butter. When done put on a dish and keep hot. Make a sauce of the drippings, and adding one tablespoon each Worcestershire sauce, walnut catsup, chopped capers and parsley. Pour some of this on the dish with the fish, and serve the rest in a bowl.

Fried Filets of Flounder.—Wash the flounder. Wipe it dry, and lay it on the table. With a sharp knife cut down to the bone in the centre of the fish, from head to tail. Lay the blade flat against the bone, and cut outwards toward the fin, and so take off the whole filet, without breaking it. Then skin each filet carefully. Lay the filet on the bread crumbs and turn till completely covered. Beat up one egg with a tablespoon of cold water. Dip the filet into the egg, and lay again on the bread. Heat enough fat until it begins to smoke. Drop the filets into it. Fry them a light brown. Take them up with a skimmer. Serve with parsley around them.

Fish Croquettes.—Remove all the skins and bones from a pound of any cold fish. Chop fine, mix with equal parts of mashed potatoes, season highly with salt and pepper, and one egg; form in small balls, roll in flour and fry brown in boiling lard. Serve hot, with walnut pickles.

Baked Codfish.—Take a cup of codfish picked fine, two cups potatoes chopped fine, one beaten egg, half cup butter, pepper; mix well and bake half an hour.

Fried Scallops.—Roll the scallops in cracker dust, then dip into the beaten yolk of one egg. Then into the cracker. Throw into hot lard, and fry like doughnuts. Dry on brown paper. Serve hot, garnished with parsley.

Clam Pie.—In a deep pie-dish lay a layer of thin-sliced potatoes, a few pieces of partially cooked onion, a few chopped raw clams, pepper and some salt (celery salt, if you like the flavor),

then another thin layer of potatoes, onions and clams, and seasoning until the dish is within an inch or so of being full; then
pour in a teacupful of the clam liquor, and fill up with hot water
until you can see it coming up between the upper pieces.   Save
the remainder of the clam liquor, if there is any left.   For crust,
use any good recipe that gives you invariably a light biscuit;
mix as usual, mould slightly and spread it with shortening quite
thickly, sprinkle on some flour, roll up and work it well; then
roll out till about three-quarters of an inch thick and the size required, cut three air holes and lay over the pie.   Put in oven;
when partly cooked, butter the crust.   Heat up your clam liquor
and add, if the broth has cooked away too much.

Oyster Pie.—Line a dish with a crisp paste, put in a layer
of oysters, salt, pepper and butter size of a walnut, half a cup of
cream, one hard boiled egg sliced, cover with grated bread crumbs,
put a little butter over them and bake brown.

Fried Oysters.—Dry them first thoroughly by draining, after-
ward laying on a napkin, covering with another until all juice is
absorbed.   To every quart allow the well-beaten yolks of two
small eggs ; stir in the oysters until they are covered; grate over
them a suspicion of nutmeg, if preferred; turn into a dish of
cracker crumbs, and toss around until well coated.   Brown in a
spider of boiling lard or butter, and salt when done, otherwise
they will not brown.

Fried Oysters.—Take fine, large oysters, put in a colander
and drain off the liquor.   Have a beaten egg on one plate and
cracker dust on another.   Lift the oysters, one at a time, with a
fork, dip first in the egg, then in the cracker dust ; lay them two
together, making them look like one, place them in the palm of
your hand and pat them together, so that they will not come
apart ; lay them on a dish until you have them all ready to fry ;
place on the fire a frying-pan, with a tablespoonful of lard, and
one of butter in it ; as soon as it is boiling hot, lay in the oysters ; sprinkle a little salt on them, and fry them a nice brown :
when done, lift them out and put them in a colander and set
them in the oven until wanted ; serve on a warm dish.

Oyster Sandwich.—Split small fresh crackers, and butter
the inside, being careful to keep those pieces which belong to-

gether side by side, as they fit much more neatly.   Lay on each
bottom half, one large, or two small oysters which you have previously examined to see that they are free from shell.   Season
with bits of butter, a little salt, and a dash of black pepper ;
cover with the upper half.   Place these prepared crackers in a
dripping-pan, and bake in a moderate oven from fifteen to twenty-
five minutes.   The cracker must be thoroughly heated through,
but not in the least burned.   Send to the table as soon as taken
from the oven.   These should be served on a hot platter, and
served with a hot pie-knife.   They are very nice to serve in the
evening with hot coffee or chocolate, and should be accompanied
by pickles.

Stewed Oysters.—Set the broth over the fire to come to a
boil.   Mix together over the fire one ounce each of butter and
flour, until they bubble.   Gradually stir this into the broth, and
season with a teaspoonful of salt, and a-quarter of a saltspoon of
white pepper.   Stir in the yolks of three raw eggs, one at a time,
and the juice of one lemon.   Put the oysters into the sauce.   Let
them heat until the edges begin to curl.   Then serve at once.

Oyster Patties.—Two eggs beaten thoroughly, one teacup
sweet milk, one teacup raw oysters chopped a little, five milk
crackers rolled fine, one teaspoon cream tartar, one-half teaspoon
of soda sifted with two tablespoons of flour, salt and pepper.
Bake on a griddle as you would griddle cakes.

Oyster Sandwiches.—Take large stewing oysters, pound
them in a mortar (having previously cut off their beards) with a
little cayenne and lemon juice.   Spread this mixture on thin
slices of brown bread and butter, cut into rounds the size of a
silver dollar.

Oyster Fritters.—Drain off the liquor from two dozen oysters and put in a sauce-pan, set on the stove.   Beat three eggs in
a cup of cream; add salt, pepper and flour to make a stiff batter,
add the oyster liquor with the oysters; fry a spoonful at a time,
dropped in boiling lard.   Serve very hot.

Escalloped Oysters.—Butter your dish, strew with bread or
cracker crumbs containing the seasoning pepper, salt and butter,
then a layer of oysters and a little milk, large piece of butter; set
in a hot oven for half an hour.

Escalloped Oysters.—Roll one pound of crackers very fine and to this add two quarts of oysters, grease an earthen baking dish sides and bottom with butter, put a layer of the cracker dust and season with butter, salt and pepper and moisten with milk warmed with a little boiling water, then a layer of oysters and season them a little, then another of crackers, season well as before, and so on till the dish is full, put the cracker dust on the top, season and moisten well, bake one hour; a little baking powder added to the cracker dust will make it lighter.

Oyster Salad.—Take a dozen and a-half of oysters; scald in their own liquor, with the addition of a-half cupful of strong vinegar, a pinch of red pepper, a pinch of white pepper and a little salt. Drain. When cold, cut the hard part of the oysters off and chop fine. Care should be taken not to hurt the appearance of the soft part of the oyster. Cut a head of celery into small dice, scraping the greenish stalks and only wipe off the white ones; mix the oysters and celery lightly together, and just before they go to the table pour over the following dressing:

DRESSING.—To the yolk of one egg beaten well add slowly, drop by drop, a wineglassful of olive oil, a pinch of mustard, salt and pepper, dissolved in a teaspoonful of vinegar, added at the last. Keep the dish and oil very cold while making. Put on ice in a cold place and pour it over the salad just before sending to table.

Fancy Roast Oysters.—Toast your bread, butter the slices and lay in a shallow dish. Put the liquor from the oysters to heat, add salt and pepper, and just before it boils add the oysters; let them boil up and pour over bread.

Pickled Oysters.—Scald the oysters in their own liquor; make some vinegar boiling hot, with some whole pepper, allspice, mace and a little salt. Take the oysters from their liquor with a bowl, and pour the hot vinegar over them. Serve celery with them. They are fit to eat as soon as cold.

Oysters and Macaroni.—Boil a-half pound of macaroni until tender. Into a deep earthen dish put a layer of the macaroni, adding small pieces of butter, a little pepper and salt. From one pint of oysters make alternate layers with the macaroni and season each layer as above. When the dish is filled pour over it the liquor from the oysters, with quarter of a pint of milk. Bake in a hot oven one-half hour, covering the dish with a pan while baking, to preserve the flavor of the oysters, but remove it five or ten minutes before they are done, and let them brown. Wrap a napkin around the dish and serve. .

Devilled Oysters is a dish too highly seasoned to find favor with many, but we give the recipe in case some would like to try it. Put a layer of raw oysters in a deep pan; then a layer of bread crumbs, black and red pepper, salt, butter, mustard and vinegar; mix together. Alternate the layers until the pan is full. Bake and serve with sliced lemon.

Oyster Sauce.—This is made of a solid pint of oysters, half a pint of chicken stock, a tablespoonful of lemon juice, four tablespoonfuls of butter; two of flour, and salt and pepper in quantities to suit the taste of the maker

PART IV.

Vegetables, Eggs, Salads, etc.

Fried Omelet.—Beat separately the whites and yolks of six eggs. Add to the yolks a tablespoonful of milk for each egg, a scant teaspoonful of salt, a dash of pepper, and, if liked, two or three tablespoonfuls of grated cheese. Stir the whites lightly into the beaten yolks and turn the whole into a hot skillet into which has been melted (care being taken not to let it brown) a tablespoonful of butter. During the frying move the skillet to and fro, shaking it gently, and if bubbles form prick them. When the omelet is nicely browned on the bottom, set it in the oven an instant to dry the top ; then fold it over with a cake turner and serve at once in a hot platter. If cheese is used, an extra tablespoonful may be sprinkled over the top before folding the omelet in half.

Plain Omelet.—Beat six eggs very thoroughly, the yolks to a cream and the whites to a stiff froth ; add to this one tablespoonful of flour or corn starch mixed smooth in one cup of sweet milk, salt and pepper and a piece of butter as large as an English walnut ; now pour this on to the white froth and without stirring at all pour the whole into a hot, buttered omelet-pan or ordinary deep frying-pan. Cook on top of stove or over a brisk fire for about five minutes and it will " rise " beautifully ; gently remove it to the hot oven and let it brown, and serve hot.

Baked Omelet.—Six eggs, whites and yolks beaten separately. Six tablespoons milk with enough flour stirred in to make a batter. Take a cup of milk, put on the stove, stir in the batter, and cook till like starch, add a piece of butter size of a walnut and a pinch of salt. Take from the stove, pour into a dish to cool, then stir in the yolks of the eggs. Beat whites to a stiff froth, add, mix well. Bake ten minutes. Eat while hot. Serve from the same dish it is baked in.

Baked Omelet.—Heat three teacupsful of milk, melting in it a bit of butter as large as a walnut. Beat well together five eggs, one teaspoonful of flour and a scant teaspoonful of salt, and add to the hot milk, stirring as rapidly as possible. Turn into a hot, well buttered frying-pan and bake in a quick oven one-quarter of an hour. Break your eggs in an earthen platter, which has been well buttered, salt them slightly and pour over a cup of cream. Will bake in a hot oven in about ten minutes.

Pickled Eggs.—Boil eggs hard, remove shells, put one spoonful each cinnamon, allspice and mace into a rag and boil in a pint of water, add vinegar enough to cover and pour over eggs.

Poached Eggs.—Place a shallow pan over the fire, half fill it with water. Add one teaspoon of salt, and two tablespoons of vinegar. Let it get scalding hot. Drop in the eggs, one by one, and let them stand five minutes without boiling. Take slices of buttered toast, and lay upon a dish. Take up the eggs, one by one, on a skimmer. Trim each evenly, and slip off on the toast. Sprinkle lightly with pepper and salt, and serve.

Ham Omelet.—Chop fine four ounces of cooked ham. Heat the omelet-pan. Put in a bit of butter the size of an English walnut. Then put in six eggs, broken separately. Then the ham. Finish as directed for plain omelet.

Oyster Omelet.—Stew half a dozen large, plump oysters over a clear fire in their own liquor, take them off at the first boil; drain them, cut them in halves and spread them over the omelet before turning. If large and solid the half dozen will suffice for two small omelets.

Celery Salad.—Stir briskly the yolk of one egg and sweet oil, by drops, until the consistency becomes stiff. Add two tablespoonsful of prepared mustard, a pinch of salt and pepper, three tablespoonsful of vinegar. Have ready three bunches of celery chopped fine, washed and well drained, then pour the above sauce over the celery.

Tomato Sauce.—Cut up fresh tomatoes and stew them in their own juice for half an hour, then put in a little onion, salt and pepper. Strain through a coarse sieve so that all will go through except the skins; then thicken with flour and add a small piece of butter. This is used as a sauce for chops, etc.

Fried Evaporated Apples.—Wash thoroughly and pick over carefully two handfuls evaporated apples; let soak twenty minutes in lukewarm water. Turn into frying-pan, add one tea-

spoon butter, and two tablespoons sugar ; spread apples to cover
pan evenly ; enough water to cover or float them.   Cover and do
not touch them until they are brown ; turn out carefully, and
serve for breakfast.   Can hardly be told from fresh apples.

Celery Toast.—Cut up stalks of celery, boil in a little water
until tender, add a little coffee, a cup of sweet milk, cook a little
longer, salt and pepper to suit the taste, thicken slightly with
flour.   Pour over toasted bread ; serve hot.

Creamed Parsnips.—While the parsnips are boiling, prepare in a double boiler a sauce of half a cupful of hot milk, thickened with a tablespoonful of butter rolled in flour and seasoned
to taste.   When smoking hot, lay the cooked parsnips, scraped
and sliced, in the sauce for five minutes, turning them two or three
times.   Serve very hot.

Fricasseed Potatoes.—Pare and slice half an inch in
thickness.   Put into cold water.   Wash well.   Put into a
sauce-pan.   Pour over them enough cold water to half cover
them.   Close the pan tightly, and let them cook fifteen minutes.
Then drain off every drop of water.   Have ready half a pint of
cream or new milk, a large spoonful of good butter, a teaspoon of
chopped parsely, and some salt.   Pour this over the potatoes,
shake them around, and just heap up.   Serve hot.

Potato Croquettes.—Mash one quart of potatoes through
a fine colander.   Mix with them one ounce of butter and the
yolks of two eggs.   Season with salt to taste, and a saltspoon of
white pepper.   Dust the board thickly with bread crumbs, and
beat up an egg with a tablespoon of water.   Dip the hands in
cold water.   Form the potatoes in little rolls, and toss them upon
the bread dust.   Dip them into the beaten egg, then into the
bread.   Fry like chicken croquettes.

Fried Apples.—Beat two eggs, add a tablespoonful of sugar
and three of sifted flour; slice tart apples, dip in the batter and
fry in butter; take up, sprinkle with sugar and serve hot.

Stewed Parsnips.—Wash and scrape the parsnips, and
slice them in pieces half an inch in thickness, then put them in a
frying-pan with half a pint of hot water and a tablespoonful of
butter.   Add salt to taste; cover closely, and let them stew until

the water is cooked out, then stir to prevent them from burning until they are a light brown color.

Macaroni a L'Italienne.—Boil the macaroni as for baked macaroni. Put the macaroni in a baking dish, in alternate layers with Parmesan cheese and canned tomatoes. Brown quickly in a hot oven. Serve hot.

Potato Pancakes.—One pint buttermilk, one egg, a little salt and soda, two teacups mashed potatoes and just enough flour to make them turn well.

Potato Pancakes.—Peel and grate, we will say, a dozen large potatoes, add about two tablespoonfuls flour, one teaspoon salt, and two eggs. Have hot grease in the frying-pan, and fry until brown. Should be eaten hot.

A Delicious Way to Cook Tomatoes.—Cut them in halves, place pulp side down in a spider with a bit of butter, for a moment or two, then turn and finish cooking without breaking the skin. Serve hot with butter, salt and pepper, like beefsteak, which in taste it resembles.

Sweet Potatoes in Sugar.—Two sweet potatoes boiled until tender, peel and cut into slices half an inch thick, sprinkle with sugar and fry in teaspoonful of hot butter to a light brown.

Celery Mayonnaise.—Cut the celery into inch pieces. Then cut the pieces into strips. Put them into a salad bowl and add plain salad dressing of oil, vinegar and mustard. Drain off the surplus dressing, and cover the celery with Mayonnaise sauce. Mix and serve.

Warm Slaw.—Take the best part of a cabbage and slice it fine, take two eggs well beaten, one cup of vinegar, one cup sweet cream, put the vinegar on the stove and when boiling hot stir in the cream and eggs, press it down with a plate, add a little salt and butter.

Green Corn Cakes.—Mix a pint of grated green corn with a teacupful of flour, half a teacupful of milk, half a teacupful of melted butter, one egg, a teaspoonful of salt and a little pepper. Drop on a buttered pan by the spoonful and bake or fry for ten or fifteen minutes.

Corn Pudding.—Four ears of corn, one pint of milk, two

eggs, butter the size of an egg, three tablespoonfuls of flour, salt and pepper. Grate the corn very fine, add the beaten eggs, milk and butter, the flour wet in a little cold milk, with the pepper and salt, beat well. Bake about an hour in a pudding dish and serve as a vegetable.

Baked Parsnips.—Scrape, and put in a deep pan with water, lay slices of pork over, and set in a slow oven over two hours; sprinkle with salt and pepper.

Tomatoes and Corn are very nice cooked together in this way. Cut the kernels from six ears of good, large, ripe corn; mix well with eight large tomatoes as for stewing. Put in three pounded crackers, season with salt and pepper and one teaspoonful of sugar, and bake half an hour in a pudding dish. The top should be covered with little strips of buttered bread which will toast nicely in the oven.

Potatoes a la Provencale.—Cut one quart of cold boiled potatoes in little balls. Chop one onion, and fry it brown in one ounce of butter. Put the potato balls into the frying-pan with the onion and butter. Shake over the fire till of a light brown. Sprinkle with salt and serve hot.

Fried Potatoes.—Take four good-sized potatoes, pare and and slice (not very thin,) have frying-pan hot, put in lump of butter, size of an egg, and put potatoes in with a pinch of salt, cover and stir from bottom of pan once or twice so they will not burn, let them brown.

Potato Saute a la Barigoule.—Cut cold boiled potatoes in the shape of olives. Toss them over the fire in hot olive oil with a tablespoonful of chopped green parsley. When brown, drain on brown paper and serve hot.

Potato Salad.—Peel and boil eight good sized potatoes. When cold, slice and lay on a flat dish a layer of the potatoes, a thin layer of finely minced onions (raw), and so on until potatoes are all used, pepper and salt. Boil two or three eggs hard, and slice over top of salad. Prepare one teaspoonful mustard with one half cup vinegar, also one-half cup melted butter, and pour over all. Eat when perfectly cold.

Mashed Potatoes.—Whip up while hot enough mealy potatoes to make a good dish. Do this with a silver fork. When fine and mealy beat in two tablespoonfuls of cream, one table-spoonful of butter, salt and pepper. Whip up into a creamy heap and mix in with a few strokes the whites of two well beaten eggs. Pile irregularly upon a buttered pie dish, spread with the beaten yolks and brown quickly in the oven.

Boiled Spinach.—Wash and pick well. Put it into a bag of coarse muslin. Pour over it plenty of hot water with a little salt in it. Boil fifteen minutes. Take it out and shake off the water. Chop it finely. Put it into a sauce-pan with a large spoonful of good butter and a little pepper. Stew it five min-utes. Dish and garnish with a hard boiled egg sliced.

Lyonnaise Potatoes—Slice a pound of cold boiled potatoes. Put two tablespoonfuls of butter in a sauce-pan with a small onion, chopped fine. Set the pan over the fire, and when the onion has fried to a delicate brown, add the potatoes, and turn and toss them till they begin to color, then stir in a little minced parsley, and serve immediately.

Scalloped Sweet Potatoes.—Boil, peel and slice. Put in a deep pan a layer of sweet potatoes and a layer of butter and sugar, until the pan is full. Set in the oven and bake brown. Sift sugar and nutmeg over the top.

A Nice Supper Dish.—One cup mashed potatoes, one cup milk, one egg, two tablespoonfuls butter; pepper and salt to taste; mix thoroughly, and bake a delicate brown.

Cabbage Salad.—One-half pint of vinegar, hot, but not boiling; stir two beaten eggs, two teaspoons sugar, one teaspoon of salt, piece of butter size of an egg, beaten all together; also two tablespoons of flour, mixed with one-half cup of milk, and stir into the hot vinegar when it commences to thicken. Take from the fire and put in a small tablespoonful of mustard, first mixing the mustard with a little water; use about one quart of cabbage chopped fine; stir the cabbage into the mixture on the stove, and cook a little without the mustard. Better to eat a day or two after making.

A Favorite Vegetable Dish.—One-third pound salt pork, one-half peck green peas, six or eight new potatoes, one-half dozen onions, two heads lettuce, a sprig of parsley; time required for cooking, three hours. Boil the pork for one hour in one quart water, then add peas and cook one hour more, when the onions and potatoes can be added. In fifteen minutes add parsley and lettuce. The lettuce must be washed carefully and tied together. Just before serving drop in a piece of butter the size of an egg, salt and pepper to suit the taste, and serve separately. The lettuce makes a most delicious dish of greens.

Baked Turnips.—Pare and slice. Boil until tender. Drain. Make a white sauce by stirring over the fire one ounce of butter and one ounce of flour, until they bubble. Stir in gradually half a pint of boiling water. Season with one saltspoonful of salt, and a quarter of a saltspoonful of pepper. Put the turnips into a baking dish, suitable to send to the table. Pour the sauce over them. Dust thickly with bread crumbs and seasonings. Brown in a quick oven.

Cauliflower.—Trim a cauliflower nicely. Let it lay in cold salted water for an hour. Let it boil about twenty minutes in boiling water, with a tablespoon of salt. Take it up carefully. Pour over it a sauce made of one ounce each of butter and flour, a gill of rich cream, and a half pint of milk. Season with pepper and salt. Sprinkle over the top a little grated cheese.

Escalloped Tomatoes.—Peel tomatoes and cut in slices one-half inch thick, then place them in a baking dish in alternate layers with bread crumbs, butter, pepper, salt and a little sugar. Bake from one-half to three-quarters of an hour.

Hot Slaw.—Break two eggs into a sauce-pan, beat thoroughly, add one teaspoon of mixed mustard, one tablespoon of sugar and one of butter, and one teacup vinegar, place over the fire and let boil, and pour hot over one head of cabbage chopped fine; just before serving salt to taste; if the salt is put in very long before it is eaten the slaw will be found to be watery.

Stuffed Potatoes.—Wash the potatoes, and bake only till they begin to soften, not more than fifteen minutes. Cut off one end. Scoop out the inside with a teaspoon into a sauce-pan containing two ounces of butter, one saltspoonful of white pepper, one teaspoonful of salt, and two ounces of grated Parmesan cheese. Stir all these over the fire till they are scalding hot.

Then fill the potato skins with the mixture. Put on the ends. Press the potatoes gently into shape. Finish baking them in the oven, and serve.

Scalloped Potatoes.—Peel raw potatoes. Slice them thin. Put a layer in baking dish, season with pepper and salt. Another layer till dish is full. Put over top a little bread crumbs and small pieces of butter. Bake one hour. Serve hot.

Egg and Spinach.—Boil and prepare some spinach. Poach some eggs, trim and lay them on the spinach. Very nice for tea.

Stewed Celery.—It is a good dish to use the roots and coarser stalks of celery as a vegetable; cut them into slices, and inch long pieces; boil till tender, and then turn off the water and pour over the celery a hot white sauce made by stirring a table-spoonful of melted butter into a heaped tablespoon of flour, and then adding to this by degrees a cup of boiling milk, stir till thickened; if the sauce becomes too thick, as it will with some flour, add more hot milk; add also salt and pepper to the sauce.

Scalloped Tomatoes.—Peel the tomatoes and prepare the same as scalloped potatoes, with the exception of putting bread crumbs between the layers as well as on top. Nicely brown in the oven. Canned tomatoes may be used in the same way.

Cold Slaw.—Two-thirds cup vinegar, one egg, two table-spoonfuls sugar, one teaspoonful salt, half teaspoonful mustard, butter size of an egg. Put on the stove, stir till it boils, then pour over the shaved cabbage when cold.

Stuffed Cabbage.—Cut out the heart of a large fresh cab-bage by gently pressing back the leaves. To do this without breaking the cabbage pour boiling water over it. Fill the hole with finely chopped veal or chicken rolled into balls with the yolk of an egg. Tie up in a cloth and boil in a covered kettle.

Tomato Shortcake.—Cook ripe tomatoes until perfectly done, after scalding and peeling them, then add a generous lump of butter, sweeten quite sweet and use the same as berries, only serve hot.

PART V.

Puddings, Delicacies, etc.

Favorite Pudding.—One-half cup sugar, one egg, two table-spoonfuls butter, one-half cup water, one and one-half cups flour, Steam one-half hour. Sauce for same. One-half cup sugar, butter size of an egg, one heaping tablespoonful flour. Rub well together, add three tablespoonsful apple jelly, any spice preferred. then slowly pour on boiling water, stirring till it thickens. Serve hot.

Peach Fritters.—Make a batter of two well-beaten eggs, one-half a pint of milk and a little salt ; pour half this mixture on a pint of flour ; beat very smooth and light and then pour in the remainder of the milk and eggs, to which is added a table-spoonful of butter or olive oil. Peel and cut the peaches in half; stir them in the batter and fry them in boiling fat until they are a delicate brown. Serve on a hot dish and sprinkle with powdered sugar.

Tapioca Cream Pudding.—Three tablespoonfuls tapioca soaked three hours in one cup of cold water. Boil one quart of milk, and add the yolks of three eggs, beaten with one cup of sugar and the tapioca. Let this cool and then cover the top with the whites of the eggs beaten with three teaspoonfuls of powdered sugar ; brown in the oven ; flavor to taste.

Fruit Puffs.—One pint flour, two teaspoonfuls baking powder, one-half teaspoonful salt. Sift all together, then stir in sweet milk till a stiff batter is formed. Put a tablespoonful of batter into teacups till half the batter is used, place on it a spoonful of any kind of canned fruit, of preserves, or of stewed apples without the juice ; preserved blue plums are nice, and color the sauce a lovely pink; put a spoonful of butter on top of the fruit in each cup ; set the cups in a steamer, and steam twenty minutes. For sauce take one-half cup sugar, two spoonfuls butter, stir to a cream, add the fruit juice and a little grated nutmeg, or the sweet cream sugar and a little nutmeg.

Dutch Pudding.—One pint flour, one cup sour milk, one egg, one-half teaspoon soda, four apples, peeled and sliced; add to the batter and stir smooth, then stir in a teaspoon of butter. Bake in shallow pan and serve with cream and sugar.

Snow Pudding.—One pint of milk, one-half cup of sugar, one-half cup of corn-starch; let come to a boil and stir in three beaten eggs. Boil till thick and set away to cool.

Cabinet Pudding. — One-half ounce of gelatine, (Peter Cooper's is best), one pint milk, three ounces powdered sugar, two ounces citron, one-fourth pound macaroons, one-fourth pound candied cherries, one lemon, one sponge cake. Soak the gelatine in two tablespoons of cold water till soft. Then put it over the fire in a sauce-pan with the sugar, milk, and rind of a lemon cut very thin. Let it heat very thoroughly. Stir occasionally until the sugar and gelatine are dissolved. Cut the citron in thin slices. Butter a pudding mould, thickly, with butter. Place the fruit and cake in alternate layers, and strain the milk into the mould. Set it in a cold place. Serve it when hard and firm.

Indian Pudding as our grandmothers made them. Boil one quart of milk, sprinkle in while hot, one-half a pint of cornmeal; have it free from lumps. Add one-half pint molasses, one teaspoon salt, lump of butter size of an egg. Mix thoroughly. Pour over all a pint of cold milk, stir well together and bake two hours in an earthen dish.

Favorite Plum Pudding.—One pint each flour, suet mixed well in flour : bread crumbs, raisins and currants, two cups dark brown sugar, spice to suit taste ; all well mixed before putting in three eggs, one-half cup sweet milk, a little water if required to make of a lumpy state, a small pinch of salt. Put in a pudding dish and tie tightly over top of dish and boil four hours.

Apple Pudding.—Make a biscuit crust, i. e., one quart of flour, three small teaspoonfuls of baking powder, butter or lard the size of an egg, teaspoonful salt, (less if butter is used), and milk enough so make a soft dough. Fill a deep baking dish with sliced apples, sweetened with molasses, and flavored with cinnamon, and pounded dried lemon peel. Cover with the crust and bake in a moderate oven.

Sago Pudding.—Steam four tablespoonfuls of sago in one quart of milk; when soft add one egg, two-thirds of a cupful of sugar, a little salt, raisins or not, according to taste.   Good, hot or cold.

Cracker Pudding.—Soak four crackers in one qurt of milk add the yolks of three eggs, three tablespoonfuls of sugar and a pinch of salt.   Flavor and bake the same as custard ; when cooked spread with canned fruit or jelly, put on a meringue made from the beaten whites of the three eggs.   Set away to cool.

Indian Pudding.—One quart of milk, half a teacup of chopped suet and five teaspoonfuls of Indian meal.   Scald half the milk and stir in the meal.   To the remainder of the milk add one egg, one tablespoonful of flour, one small teacup of molasses, one small teaspoonful ginger, and one cup of raisins; mix together ; bake slowly two hours ; serve hot.

Apple Dumplings.—Take some finely sifted flour, say one-half pound, and half the quantity of suet, one-fourth pound, very finely shred, and well freed from skin.   Mix the suet and flour, add a pinch of salt, and a-half teaspoonful baking powder, with sufficient cold water or milk to make it of the right consistency.   Knead it well, and roll it out to the thickness required. Divide this paste into as many pieces as are required for the dumplings.   Take some large-sized apples, peel, core, sprinkle them with moist sugar, then insert into the cavity of each some butter, sugar and cloves.   Cover them with the paste, and join the edges carefully.   Tie each dumpling up in a floured cloth, and boil about an hour.   Untie them carefully, and turn them out without breaking them.   Serve with cream and sugar.   A little currant jelly may be substituted for the butter, sugar and clove.

Rice Pudding.—One-half cup of rice, one and a-half pints milk, one-half cup of sugar, large pinch of salt, one tablespoonful lemon rind chopped fine.   Put rice washed and picked, sugar, salt and milk in a quart pudding dish.   Bake in a moderate oven two hours, stirring frequently first one and a-quarter hours, then permit it to finish cooking with light colored crust. Eat with cream.

Indian Pudding.—Take one pint milk, one-half cup molasses, two-thirds cup meal, scald the milk and stir into the others with a little salt, then add the rest of the milk cold.   I put this in the oven after breakfast and let cook slowly till supper time, then it comes out looking red and all jellied.

Delicate Indian Pudding.—One quart of milk scalded, two heaping tablespoonfuls of meal, cook twelve minutes; stir into this one tablespoonful of butter, then beat three eggs with four tablespoonfuls of sugar, one half tablespoonful of ginger, salt to taste, mix all thoroughly, and bake one hour.

Cooking Rice.—One cup of rice, one and one-half cups boiling water, little salt, boil rapidly, well covered, set on back of stove and steam one-half hour or more.

Puff Pudding.—One pint of sweet milk, four eggs, four tablespoons flour, mix flour with just enough milk to beat smoothly, gradually stirring in until all the milk is mixed, beat the yolks, then slowly pour the mixture into the yolks, beating all the time, lastly, the whites well beaten; bake in a quick oven. Eat with hard or wine sauce.

Rasin Puffs.—Two eggs, one-half cup butter, three teaspoonfuls baking powder, two tablespoonfuls sugar, two cups flour, one cup chopped raisins; steam one-half hour in small cups.

Potato Starch Pudding.—To one quart of milk boiling hot, put four tablespoonfuls of potato starch, three eggs, and a little salt well mixed and beaten together, and your pudding is made. To be served with rich sauce.

Baked Indian Meal Pudding.—Take one cup of meal, moisten with cold water, then pour on one pint of boiling water, while this is cooling take two eggs, one cup sugar, beat, add butter the size of an egg, then stir together and add sweet milk according to family.

Steamed Pudding.—One-half cup of molasses, two-thirds cup of browned sugar, one-half cup of butter, one cup sour milk, two level teaspoons of soda, one quart of flour, one cup of raisins, spices, any sauce can be used to suit the taste; steam one and one-half hours.

Cocoanut Pudding.—Carefully grate one cocoanut. Beat to a cream one pound of powdered sugar and half a pound of good butter. Beat the whites of eleven eggs to a stiff froth. Stir the cocoanut, butter and sugar well together. Add one wine glass of rose water, one wine glass of wine and brandy mixed. Beat this mixture well. Grate one-half a rind of a lemon.

Lastly add the whites of the eggs. Have a baking dish lined with paste and bake half an hour. Paste.—One cup of lard, one-half cup of water, one-half teaspoon salt. The above is a delicious pie crust.

Apple Fritters.—Make a batter of the yolks of three eggs well beaten, one gill milk, four heaping tablespoonfuls flour and a saltspoonful salt, well mixed. The apples, which have been peeled, cored and cut in round slices, are dipped in this batter and fried a delicate brown in boiling fat; sprinkle with powdered sugar and serve.

Lemon Rice Pudding.—One cup boiled rice, one pint milk, grated rind of a lemon, butter size of an egg, yolks of three eggs; bake twenty minutes; frost with the whites of the eggs, beaten with one-half pound white sugar and juice of the lemon; add just after taking from the oven; return and brown lightly; moderate oven; very nice.

Pineapple Pudding.—Line a deep and buttered pudding dish with slices of sponge cake ; slice some pineapple in very thin slices and put it into the dish ; cover a layer of pineapple with a layer of cake, and so on until the dish is full ; scatter sugar plentifully over the pineapple ; the top layer of cake should be moistened with water and have sugar scattered over it. If you are the happy possessor of a pudding-dish with an earthen cover, put this over the pudding, otherwise cover it with a dinner plate and bake slowly one and three-fourths hours. The cover or plate should be buttered.

Indian Custard Pudding.—One quart new milk, four teaspoons fine Indian meal, one egg, salt, spice and sweeten to taste; beat the eggs and meal together, pour in the milk, stir twice while baking.

Corn-starch Custard.—Six tablespoonfuls of corn-starch boiled in one quart of milk, sugar to taste, peel of two lemons grated and the juice of one. When thick, pour into a wetted dish. Beat one cup of sugar with the whites of five eggs and pour over the corn-starch; set in the oven until slightly browned. Serve hot or cold with a custard made of the yolks of the eggs.

Frozen Pudding.—Ingredients : One and one-half pints of custard, composed of the yolks of four eggs, a pint of boiled milk, four tablespoonfuls of sugar, a flavoring of vanilla, eight ounces of fruits, consisting of equal parts of dried cherries, pineapple, dried pears or apricots, all cut into very small squares. These fruits may be selected, or perhaps it would be more convenient to purchase half a pound of the French preserved dried fruits ; or add one ounce of candied citron sliced, two ounces of currants, two ounces of chopped raisins, and half a pint of cream, whipped. Freeze the custard in the usual manner, then mix in the fruits and whipped cream. Put into a mould, and place it on ice and sa't. Serve with whipped cream.

Baked Apple Pudding.—Fill earthen pudding-dish with pared and quartered apples. Prepare a crust of sweet cream, a very little soda and salt. Cover the apples, and put them in to bake one hour before dinner. It can be eaten with sugar or any kind of pudding sauce.

Virginia's Plum Pudding.—One cup of molasses, one teaspoonful soda, mix it into it well; one cup of suet chopped fine, or three-fourths of a cup of butter, one cup of milk, one teaspoonful of cloves, cinnamon, and nutmeg, one cup of raisins, currants and citron, three cups of flour, a little salt ; boil about five hours.

Farmers' Pudding.—Two eggs, one cup sweet milk, one pint flour, two tablespoons each melted butter and sugar, two teaspoons baking powder. Steam from twenty to twenty-five minutes, and serve with sauce.

Prune Pudding.—Scald one pound French prunes, let them swell in hot water until soft; extract stones; spread on a dish and dredge with flour; take a gill of milk from one quart, stir in gradually eight tablespoonfuls sifted flour; beat six eggs light, and stir by degrees into remainder of the quart of milk, alternating with the batter; add prunes, one at a time, stir very hard, boil two hours and serve with cream or wine sauce.

Southern Potato Pudding.—One pint of grated raw potatoes, one-half pound brown sugar, one-quarter pound butter, two eggs; stir constantly while baking, when done leave in stove long enough to brown a little.

Steamed Pudding.—Half cup each sugar and butter, three eggs, one cup sweet milk, three heaping teaspoons baking powder, two cups flour. Steam one hour, serve with sauce.

Puff Pudding —Eight eggs, one quart sweet milk, eight tablespoonfuls of flour, wet the flour with enough milk to beat smooth, then gradually stir in the whole quart, beat the yolks and stir them in slowly, then lastly the whites; bake in buttered dish. Eat with hard sauce.

Tapioca Pudding.—Take ten tablespoonfuls of tapioca, wash it in warm water, drain off the water, and put the tapioca in a pan with a quart of rich milk, set the pan over a kettle of boiling water and stir it till it thickens, then add two tablespoons of butter, six of white sugar, one grated lemon or flavor to suit the taste with good lemon or vanilla extract; remove the pan from the fire, and having beaten four eggs very light stir them gradually into the mixture, pour it into a buttered dish and bake three-fourths of an hour. Serve with rich cream or custard sauce.

Pop Overs.—Two cups sweet milk, two cups sifted flour, two eggs, two teaspoons butter, one-half teaspoonful salt; beat eggs, add milk, then the flour and salt and after beating thoroughly stir in the butter which has been melted, use no soda or baking powders. Have the oven hot, bake in well-buttered roll pans (which should be heated) about one-half hour.

French Tapioca Pudding.—Two ounces of tapioca, one-half pint of water, one-half pint of milk, one well-beaten egg, one teaspoonful of lemon extract. Boil the tapioca in the water until it begins to melt and then slowly add the milk, egg and flavoring. Bake for twenty minutes.

Cottage Pudding.—Two eggs, one cup sweet milk, two tablespoons of sugar, two tablespoons of melted butter, one pint of flour, two teaspoons of baking powder, flavor with nutmeg. Steam one hour and serve with sweetened cream.

Rice Meringue Pudding.—Put a teacup of rice in a pint of water. When the water is boiled away, add a pint of milk, a piece of butter the size of an egg, the yolks of three eggs and the grated rind of one lemon. Mix well. Pour into a pudding dish, spread over the top the whites of the eggs beaten to a stiff froth with a teacup of sugar. Set in the oven and brown a little.

Mountain Snow Pudding.—One and a-half pints milk, two milk crackers rolled, beaten yolks of three eggs; flavor, and bake twenty minutes, then spread the beaten whites and three table-spoons sugar over the top, and return to the oven until slightly browned. Very nice and delicate.

Brown Betty.—Place in a pudding-dish first a layer of finely sliced apples, sugared to taste and dusted over with powdered cinnamon, next a layer of coarsely crumbed bread, scattered with bits of butter. Alternate these layers until the dish is full, letting the last layer consist of apples. Pour on sufficient water to moisten the whole, cover, and place in the oven. When the apples on the top are tender, remove the cover and bake until brown. Serve hot, without sauce.

Chocolate Pudding.—One quart of milk, three ounces of chocolate, grated; four eggs, one cup of sugar, two teaspoonfuls of vanilla. Boil milk with chocolate; when dissolved, take from fire and add yolks of eggs, beaten well with sugar. Bake like custard in a dish of hot water; when cold frost with the whites and brown; to be eaten cold.

Berry Pudding.—One cup molasses, one cup milk, one egg, one teaspoonful cream tartar, one teaspoonful soda; flour to make a stiff batter, and berries. Steam one and one-half or two hours.

Sponge Pudding.—Use three-quarter cup of flour, one-half cup of sugar, one pint sweet milk, six eggs, beaten separately. Blend the flour with a little of the milk, put the rest with the sugar on the stove until it begins to boil, then add the blended flour. Have the yolks well beaten in the dish you are to bake it in. Pour the hot mixture on it, blend thoroughly, then add the beaten whites. Set the dish in a pan of water and bake from one-half to a quarter of an hour. Serve with liquid sauce.

Steamed Pudding.—Two eggs, one cupful sugar, one cupful sour milk, one-half teaspoonful soda and three cupfuls flour; one cupful of fruit if you like. Steam two hours. To be eaten with sweetened cream or sauce.

Baked Indian Pudding.—Five tablespoonfuls of Indian meal, two tablespoonfuls of flour, two eggs, one cup of molasses, one teaspoonful of salt. Mix well together and pour on one quart of boiling milk. When mixed well together pour in one quart of cold milk, but do not stir it.

Steamed Indian Pudding.—Three cupfuls of Indian meal,

a cupful of flour, three cupfuls of sweet milk, a cupful of sour milk, three-fourths cupful of molasses, a teaspoonful of soda dissolved in the sweet milk, the flour and meal stirred together to prevent lumps, a teaspoonful of salt; steam four hours, and eat with hot butter or cream sweetened a little, and flavored with nutmeg.

Rhubarb Pudding is made in this way. Use an earthen dish and line with slices of bread and butter, cover with cut up rhubarb, over which put a layer of sugar, then another layer of bread and butter, then rhubarb and sugar, and so on until the dish is full, having the top layer rhubarb and sugar. Cover tightly and bake half an hour. Serve while warm with a sweet sauce.

Cracker Pudding.—A plain but very nice pudding. Soak in one quart warm milk, one pint cracker crumbs, add yolks two beaten eggs, one-half cup sugar, small piece butter, pinch salt (nutmeg or without, to suit taste); bake one-half hour; beat whites of two eggs to a froth, add two tablespoonfuls sugar and flavor with lemon, spread on pudding, brown in oven.

Fried Bananas.—Take firm bananas, peel and slice, sprinkle with a little salt, dip the slices in a thin batter and fry in butter. Must be eaten hot.

Orange Ambrosia. — Take two large oranges, peel and slice ; put in a deep glass dish a layer of orange and sprinkle with sugar. Then add a layer of grated cocoanut and again sprinkle with sugar; keep on until all is used, finishing with a thin layer of cocoanut ; buy a cocoanut and grate it, which is cheaper than using the prepared.

Velvet Cream.—Soak one-half box gelatine in a cup of cold water, scald one quart of milk, beat the yolks of five eggs with ten tablespoonfuls sugar. Add all to milk and boil, beat whites to froth, and stir in when cool ; add two tablespoonfuls wine and one of vanilla. Pour into moulds and set away to freeze.

Banana Pudding.—Place a layer of cake, then of bananas, in a dish, until nearly full, leaving bananas on top. Then make a custard of three eggs, a pint of milk, and pour over them. Whip cream and put on top.

Trifle.—Take slices of cake, and place in the bottom of a glass dish. Pour over it whipped cream. First dip the cake in sherry.

Lemon Jelly.—Juice and grated rind of one lemon, one large sour apple grated, one egg, one cup sugar. Stir constantly till it boils.

Lemon Jelly.—One lemon, one cup of sugar, one egg, one tablespoonful cold water, grate the rind, squeeze out the juice, beat all together and boil until it thickens.

Orange Jelly (French).—Swell two ounces of gelatine in two quarts of cold water, with twelve spoonfuls of sugar, and the whites of two eggs beaten to a froth ; strain through a wet napkin into an earthen dish ; add the rind of four very fair oranges, pared very thin ; cover, and partly cool ; add the juice of eight oranges and two lemons ; strain, and mix with the other ingredients. A few drops of yellow coloring is an improvement. It is then ready for cooling.

Apple Compote.—This is a delicious dish. Cut up, skins and all, six apples and boil in one pint water until apples are soft. Drain off the juice, and add to it one cup sugar, and a little grated lemon rind (only the yellow, none of the white, ever). Boil this mixture one minute, put six apples pared and cored (with a patent corer that leaves the apples whole) into the sauce thus prepared and cook until tender. Then remove the apples, and fill centres with orange marmalade. Boil the sauce in which they were cooked until it jellies, and pour it over the apples. This is an ornamental dish when daintily served, and most delicious to the taste.

Coffee Jelly.—One-half box gelatine dissolved in one-half cup of cold water, two hours, pour over this one pint boiling coffee; stir thoroughly, add one cup sugar when this is dissolved, pour over one-half cup boiling water.

Blanc Mange.—Four tablespoons of corn-starch to one quart of milk, beat the corn-starch thoroughly with two eggs, and add to it the milk when near boiling, with a little salt, boil a few minutes stirring it briskly, flavor to taste and pour into a mould ; sweeten while cooking or use a sauce of cream and sugar. To be eaten cold.

Orange Pudding. — One quart milk, three tablespoonfuls corn-starch, yolks four eggs, one-half cup sugar. Pare and slice the oranges, and place in a dish in layers alternately with sugar, make a custard of the other ingredients and pour over them. Beat the whites of the eggs and three tablespoonfuls of sugar together, put on top, and set in the oven to brown. Peaches may be used the same way.

Wine Jelly. — Dissolve in a little warm water, one ounce isinglass, add a pint of port wine, two ounces sugar, one ounce gum arabic and one-half nutmeg grated, mix all well, then boil ten minutes or until dissolved, strain and set away to cool.

Snow Pudding. — Soak half a box of gelatine (white) in half pint warm water until it is dissolved ; then add half pint boiling water, when cold add the whites of three eggs, two cups sugar, juice of one large lemon, beat the whole well, one-half hour will not be too long, and put in a mould to cool. Make a boiled custard and the yolks and a pint of sweet milk, sweeten to taste and pour over the pudding. It is good, as well as very pretty.

Corn-starch, Blanc Mange and Chocolate Sauce. — Take two tablespoonfuls of corn-starch and mix with cold milk very smooth ; warm to boiling point two points of milk, in which some lemon rind, sugar and a few drops of essence had been put and pour into the corn-starch without the lemon peel, while stirring all the time. Let simmer a few minutes while stirring, and pour into a shape. Melt a little fresh butter in sauce-pan, stir in half a spoon of corn flour and some chocolate finely scraped, with sugar to taste, pour in warm milk, stirring all the time, and beat up with the yolk of an egg. Having turned out the blanc mange at serving, pour the chocolate sauce over it.

Apricot Cream. — Take a jar of preserved apricots. Turn out the contents into a sauce-pan. Add two ounces of sugar. Let them boil for a-quarter of an hour. Pass them through a tammy. Dissolve an ounce of gelatine in a little cold milk. Whip to a froth a pint of cream. Mix the gelatine with the apricot pulp, then quickly work into it the cream. Pour the mixture into a mould, and put it on the ice to set.

Tapioca Cream. — Soak three tablespoonfuls of tapioca in a pint of cold water over night. In the morning drain, put the tapioca, yolks three eggs, well beaten, and a large three-fourths cup of sugar into one quart of boiling milk. Let it all boil a few minutes, then take from the fire. Flavor with lemon or vani la. Beat the whites of the eggs and mix through. Pour in a dish to cool.

Boiled Custard.—One quart of milk, the yolks of four eggs, four large tablespoonfuls of powdered or granulated sugar, one teaspoonful of wheat flour, a small pinch of salt; beat the eggs, sugar and flour together, thinning it with a little of the milk: boil the milk and pour it while boiling on the eggs, etc., stirring it, and return it to the skillet; keep stirring it carefully until the eggs are thoroughly cooked; after pouring into bowl, continue stirring until nearly cold, then flavor to taste. The whites of the eggs beaten very light with any well flavored firm fruit jelly, and dropped in spoonfuls over the custard, make a very palatable dish.

A Nice Dessert.—Soak two cups of bread or crackers in water, squeeze dry; add the yolks of three well beaten eggs, one-half cup sugar, cinnamon to taste; stir well, then add the whites of three eggs. Fry in small cakes in hot lard or butter. Should be served hot with stewed prunes.

Spanish Cream.—One quart milk, four eggs, one-half box gelatine. Pour half the milk on gelatine and let it stand an hour; add the rest of the milk, and boil all together. Separate the eggs, adding twelve tablespoons sugar to the beaten yolks and four to the whites. When the milk and gelatine have boiled add the yolks. When the cream is thick and smooth, take off the fire and let it get quite cool, then add the whites. Use vanilla, or a little wine gives it a good flavor.

Neapolitan Blanc Mange.—Heat one pint milk, stir in two tablespoonfuls corn-starch dissolved in a little milk, two tablespoonfuls sugar, letting it boil a few minutes, add strawberry coloring. Set away to cool. Heat another pint and make the same way, using vanilla for flavoring, and to a third pint grated chocolate. When cool put together in layers so when dipped out there will be the three colors, which makes a very pretty dish served.

Snow, Ice and Thaw.—Put one-half package of gelatine in a little cold water, then pour over one pint of boiling water, when cool add the juice of two lemons, and a scant pint of sugar, when cold add the whites of two eggs well beaten. Beat all to a stiff fro h, pour into moulds and let it stand till next day. Make a soft custard of one egg and the yolks of three, one cup sugar and one pint milk. Beat up the whites of the eggs with sugar, and put over the top.

Bananas and Cream.—Slice eight or ten bananas thin into a glass dish, sprinkle with powdered sugar, then pour over a cupful of whipped cream and serve with cake.

Ice Cream.—Four eggs, one quart milk, one tablespoonful corn-starch, six tablespoonfuls sugar. Boil in a pan over a kettle of water, flavor and freeze.

White Mountain for Dessert.—Three cups milk, four eggs, one cup sugar, one small tablespoon corn-starch or flour, and one teaspoon extract lemon; put milk on stove to boil, beat the whites with three tablespoons white sugar, one teaspoon lemon; put them in the boiling milk to cook, turn them with a large ladle, and lift carefully out; beat the yolks, sugar and starch smooth, stir in milk, let boil, take from stove and stir in one teaspoon lemon· cool so as not to break the dish; put in dish, and put on top the cooked whites. Keep in a cool place until wanted; set on table, and sprinkle red sugar over top.

Macedoine of Fruits.—One-fourth pound of candied grapes, one-fourth pound of candied oranges, one-fourth pound of candied cherries, one-fourth pound of candied currants, one-half pint of wine jelly, one-half pint of currant jelly, one-half pint of lemon jelly, one-half pint of orange jelly. Melt each jelly separately. Pour the wine jelly into a mould. Set away to become hard. Then put the oranges on top of it, and the currant jelly on top of that. Let it set. When firm, put on it the grapes, and on top of that pour the lemon jelly. When firm pile on the cherries. Lastly pour over the orange jelly, and pile with the currants. Set upon the ice, till perfectly firm. Turn out and serve.

V's Cup Custards.—Yolks of four eggs, four tablespoonsful of sugar, one pint of milk, warm the milk, beat eggs and sugar together, stir into the warm milk a little vanilla, put into cups, add nutmeg, put cups into a pan of warm water and bake in a slow oven.

A Nice Dish of Apples.—One pint of the pulp of roasted apples, strained; one-half pint of pulverized sugar; the whites of three eggs. Beat the whites of the eggs to a stiff froth, then add a spoonful of apple, and a spoonful of sugar alternately, beating all together until the mixture stands perfectly stiff on the spoon. It will swell very much. Make a boiled custard of the three yolks of eggs, one pint of milk, two tablespoonfuls of sugar, and flavor with vanilla. Place the custard in saucers, and cover with the apple sauce, and serve.

Lemon Cream.—Take the grated rinds and juice of three lemons with three-quarters of a pound of sugar; add to a box of Cox's gelatine dissolved in a pint of sherry wine. Stir it well over the fire, then strain and stir it carefully into a quart of cream. Mould when cool. For orange cream substitute three juicy oranges and add a wineglass of brandy.

Prune Whip.—Sweeten and stew three-quarters of a pound of prunes; when perfectly cold add the whites of four eggs beaten stiff; stir together and bake twenty minutes; when cold serve to be eaten with cream.

Caramel Custard.—One quart of new milk, six eggs, one cupful brown sugar, one cupful white sugar, a teaspoonful and a half of vanilla. While the milk is heating put the brown sugar in a hot spider and stir till it is quite brown; add this to the hot milk, and proceed as with any custard. When thick, strain and set in a cool place. It is nicest when made the day before using.

Salted Peanuts.—Shell the peanuts or almonds, remove the skins, put in a dripping pan with just enough butter to make them glossy and then brown them in a hot oven, shaking the pan frequently to make them brown evenly, when the nuts are brown sprinkle them with salt.

Chocolate Jelly.—Take seven spoonfuls of grated chocolate, the same of white sugar, one cup of sweet cream; mix together and set over the fire and let come to a boil. Pour it over cornstarch pudding, or put between layers of cake.

PART VI.

Cakes.

Orange Cake.—Teacup of sugar, one-half cup butter, one-half cup of water, two cups flour, two teaspoonfuls baking powder, yolks of three eggs, juice of an orange. Bake in four tins like Washington pie, and place one above the other with the following icing spread between : Teacup granulated sugar, one-half cup boiling water. Boil until a little dropped in water will harden and can be rolled into a ball. Beat the whites of two eggs to a froth, pour the syrup on the eggs, slowly beating all the time until the mixture is creamy. Add the juice and grated rind of an orange and spread. Be careful not to cook the syrup too much. It will be coarse if cooked longer than necessary.

Orange Cake.—Two cups sugar, one-half cup butter, four eggs, juice of two oranges, and grated peel of one, the grated peel of half a lemon, three cups of flour, one teaspoon baking powder. Mix the juice and peel with the sugar, add the butter, then the yolks, and lightly sift in the flour, whisk in the white of the egg, and hurry the cake into the oven. Bake in three cakes. Between each layer and on top spread frosting made of the whites of two eggs, two cups of sugar, and the grated peel and juice of one small orange.

Orange Cake.—Two cups sugar, one and one-half cups melted butter, one cup of milk, three cups of flour, yolks of four eggs, white of three, two teaspoons baking powder, grated rind of orange. Filling.—White of one egg, juice of two oranges, rinds of two, sugar to make thick enough to spread smooth. Bake in two tins and spread filling between and on the top.

Excellent Orange Cake.—Two cups of sugar, half a cup of water that has been boiled, yolks of five eggs, two cups of flour, grated rind and juice of one orange, one teaspoonful of cream of tartar, a half teaspoonful of soda and a litt'e salt ; bake in layer. Icing for the cake : Beat the reserved whites of four eggs to a froth, stir in powdered sugar until quite stiff, add grated rind and juice of an orange. Put the cakes together with this. If you wish to cover the top of the cake with the icing make stiffer with powdered sugar.

Cocoanut Cake.—Two eggs, two cups of sugar, two table-spoonfuls of butter, one cup of sweet milk, two teaspoonfuls of cream of tartar, one teaspoonful of soda, one and one-half cups of flour, flavor to taste. Take the white of one egg, beat to a stiff froth, add one-half cup of granulated sugar, spread between the layers and on top, and sprinkle with grated cocoanut.

Cocoanut Cake.—One cup of sugar, one-half cup of butter, two eggs, one cup of milk, one and one-half teaspoonfuls baking powder, two cups of flour, bake in layers. Filling.—Boil one pint of milk, add when boiling a-half cup of Schepp's cocoanut, take a tablespoonful of corn-starch, two of sugar, one egg, beat all together, in a-half cup of cold milk and then stir in the boiling milk, when cool spread between layers.

Cocoanut Cake.—One cup sugar, half cup butter, one egg and yolks of two, half cup milk, two cups flour, half teaspoon cream tartar, quarter teaspoon soda, flavor with lemon, bake in two layers. Filling.—Beat two whites to a froth, two tablespoons sugar, spread between and on top, sprinkle with cocoanut.

Cocoanut Cake.—Two cups sugar, three cups flour, two-thirds cup butter, one cup sweet milk, whites of five eggs, two teaspoons baking powder. Bake in layers. For filling.—One pint sweet milk, one-half cup sugar, one egg, three teaspoonfuls corn-starch, cook thoroughly, stir in one grated cocoanut.

May's Cocoanut Cake.—The whites of six eggs, two cups of powdered sugar, three-fourths of a cup of butter, one cup of sweet milk, three cups of flour, two teaspoonfuls of baking powder, one of lemon essence, spread this cake top and sides with cocoanut icing when done.

Nut Cake.—Two and one-half cups of sugar, one cup of butter, one cup of milk, four cups of flour, four eggs, whites and yolks beaten separately, three teaspoons of baking powder. This makes three layers and six small round cakes. For Summer only use three-fourths of a cup of butter. Between the layers.— Whites of two eggs, one tablespoon of powdered sugar to an egg well beaten, one coffee cup of chopped hickory nuts. Frost the top with plain frosting and lay on whole meats. English walnuts can be used instead.

Hickory Nut Cake.—Two eggs, one cup sugar, one-half cup each of butter and sweet milk, one cup flour, one teaspoon baking powder and one cup of hickory nut meats or any other kind of nuts.

Nut Cake.—One cup butter, two cups sugar, four eggs, one cup milk, two teaspoons baking powder, sifted through with three cups flour, one and a-half cups shagbark meats. Frost the top, and before marking it off put rows of English walnut meat (broken in halves) across on every side.

Nut Cake.—One cup sugar, half cup butter, half cup milk, two cups flour, two eggs, one cup chopped raisins, one cup chopped English walnuts, one teaspoonful cream tartar, one-half teaspoonful soda.

Chocolate Cake.—One cup of sugar, one-half cup of butter, two eggs, one-half cup of milk, one-half teaspoonful of soda, one teaspoonful cream tartar, two cups flour. The cream is made thus: One-third cake of chocolate, one-half cup of milk, yolk of one egg, sugar to taste; boil until stiff; when cold spread over the cake.

Chocolate Cake.—One cup butter, two of sugar, five eggs, (leaving out the whites of two), one cup sweet milk, one teaspoon cream tartar, one half of soda, both dissolved in milk, three and one-half cups of flour, scant measure. For frosting take the whites of two eggs, one and one-half cups of powdered sugar, six large tablespoons grated chocolate, two teaspoons vanilla; frost while the cake is hot.

Chocolate Cake.—Two cups of sugar, one cup of milk, three cups of flour, one-half cup of butter, three teaspoons of baking powder, three eggs, two teaspoonfuls of vanilla, make four layers. Filling.—Two squares of chocolate grated, one cup of pulverized sugar, one-half cup of boiling milk, stir all together and add one heaping teaspoonful of corn-starch stirred in a little cold milk. Flavor with vanilla.

Chocolate Marble Cake.—One cup of butter, two cups of sugar, one of sweet milk, three of flour, whites of five eggs, three teaspoonfuls of baking powder. Take out one teacupful of the batter, add to it five tablespoons of grated chocolate, moistened with vanilla. Pour a layer of the white batter into the baking-pan, then drop the chocolate batter with a spoon in spots and spread the remainder of the white batter over it.

Chocolate Cake.—Two cups sugar, half-cup butter, three eggs, one cup milk, three cups flour, two teaspoons baking powder; bake in jelly tins. Make caramel as follows: Butter size of an egg, pint brown sugar, half a cup milk or water, half a cake chocolate; boil until thick enough and pour over cakes while warm.

Chocolate Cake.—Whites of four eggs, two cups of sugar, one-half cup of butter, one cup of sweet milk, three cups of flour, two teaspoons of baking powder. Filling: One cup chocolate, one cup sugar, one cup milk, yolks of four eggs.

Chocolate Cake.—Two cups sugar, one-half cup of butter, one cup milk, three cups flour, one teaspoon cream of tartar, one-half teaspoon soda, two eggs; take two squares chocolate grated, dissolve in a little boiling water, one-half cup sugar, add three large spoonfuls cake dough, mix well and marble. Chocolate frosting.

Chocolate Cake.—One cup sugar, one-half cup butter, beaten to a cream, the whites of four eggs, whipped stiff, one-half cup sweet milk, one heaping teaspoonful of baking powder, mixed in one good cup of flour. Take half of the mixture and grate in one square of chocolate, add one teaspoon of vanilla, then dip together the same as marble cake.

Raised Cake.—One heaping pint bowl of bread dough as soon as it is ready to mould into loaves, four eggs beaten separately, one cup butter, two cups sugar, two tablespoons cinnamon, one nutmeg, one-half teaspoon soda, one pint bowl of stoned raisins, mix by hand; put the dough in a large bowl; first work in the butter, then the sugar and spice, next the yolks of the eggs, then the beaten whites, then the soda dissolved in a little warm water, and lastly the raisins. Bake in two loaves after raising fifteen minutes.

Loaf Cake.—Three cups of milk, two cups of sugar, and one and one-third cups of lard and butter mixed or all lard.

whites of three eggs, one yeast cake. Make a sponge of yeast first. Stir in flour as thick as you can with a spoon. Rise over night. Add in the morning the sugar, lard, eggs, together with raisins, two nutmegs, citron, and brandy. Work all together, and rise again. Then put into pans and bake, leaving the oven open just a few moments. This makes four loaves.

Buttermilk Cake.—Four eggs, two cups sugar, one cup butter, one cup sour or buttermilk, teaspoon soda, four cups sifted flour, cream butter and sugar together, then add the eggs well beaten and milk and last flour, beat well, do not stir. Bake in moderate oven.

Lemon Cake.—Two cups of sugar, one-half cup butter, three eggs, three cups flour, two teaspoonfuls of baking powder. Jelly for cake.—The rinds of two lemons, juice of same, one cup of sugar, one egg, one-half cup of water, one teaspoonful of butter, one tablespoonful of flour ; mix the latter with a little water, boil till a little thick and spread between cakes when cool.

Caramel Cake.—For the cake : Two eggs, one cup of sugar, one-half cup of butter, one-half cup of milk, two cups of flour, one teaspoon of cream tartar, one-half teaspoon of soda. Bake in layers. Filling : One cup of sugar, the white of one egg and one large sour apple, pared and grated ; beat all together until you can turn the dish upside down, then spread on top and between the layers.

Layer Cake.—One cup sugar, two eggs, two-thirds cup of milk, three tablespoonfuls butter, two cups flour, two teaspoonfuls baking powder. For the filling, one cup each of walnut meats and raisins chopped in frosting, with half meats of English walnuts on top. Try this and see how pretty and good it is.

Fig Layer Cake.—One cup sugar, three even tablespoons of butter, one egg and the yolks of two, two-thirds of a cup of milk, two cups of flour, one teaspoon of soda, two of cream tartar, bake in three layers. Fig paste : One cup sugar, one-fourth cup water, boil till thick ; test by dropping a little in cold water, like candy ; beat the white of one egg to a stiff froth ; chop eight figs very fine, take the sugar from the stove, cool five minutes, add the white of egg, beat five minutes and add the figs. Spread on the cake ; delicious.

Date Cake.—Make a plain loaf cake as follows: One and one-half cups sugar, two eggs, reserving white of one for frosting, butter size of an egg, one cup water, two heaping teaspoons baking powder and flour to mix rather soft. Prepare dates by washing and removing stones, cut each one in four pieces, flour well and stir in cake. Bake quickly in middling hot oven.

Pineapple Cake.—One cup of butter, two cups sugar, one cup of milk, three cups of flour, whites of six eggs and yolks of four, three teaspoonfuls of baking powder well mixed through flour; bake in layers, grate a pineapple, sprinkle with sugar, spread between the layers, pineapple jam may be substituted; frost the outside, beat two tablespoonfuls of pineapple into the frosting.

Banana Cake.—One cup butter, small cup sweet milk, two cups sugar, two teaspoons baking powder, three cups flour. Bake in layers, spread the whites of four eggs. Boiled frosting between layers. Slice bananas (three good sized ones) thin and distribute over frosting and sprinkle fine white sugar over bananas.

Banana Cake.—Half cup butter, two cups sugar, three cups flour, three eggs, one cup sweet milk, one and one-half teaspoonfuls of baking powder. Mixture for cake between layers: Two cups sugar, one-fourth cup of water, whites of two eggs beaten to a stiff froth, boil the sugar and water till it threads, then pour over the beaten whites and beat until cold; spread icing on each layer and on top of icing the slices of three large bananas.

Ribbon Cake.—Three eggs, one and one-half cups of sugar, one-half cup of butter, two-thirds cup of sweet milk, three cups of flour, and two heaping teaspoonfuls of baking powder, mix all thoroughly, take out one-third for the dark loaf, add to it one-half cup of raisins, two tablespoonfuls of molasses and spices to taste; bake the light in two loaves, the dark in one and put together with jelly or frosting.

Ribbon Cake.—One cup of sugar, three-fourths cup of butter, two cups of flour, three teaspoonfuls of baking powder, whites of five eggs, mixed. Take from this mixture a large tablespoon of batter, to this add one-half cup of chopped raisins, one-half cup chopped citron, one-half cup flour, one-half cup molasses, two teaspoonfuls of cinnamon, one-half teaspoonful of cloves, one wine-glass of brandy. Bake in layers like jelly cake with frosting between one layer of the light batter and one layer of the dark. Place a pan of water in the stove while baking to keep the cake soft.

Harlequin Cake.—Take one cup sugar, two tablespoonfuls of butter, two-thirds cup of milk, whites of three eggs beaten to a stiff froth, two teaspoonfuls of baking powder, two small cups flour. After mixing this, divide into three parts, leaving one of the parts white; add to one part the yolks of two eggs, and one tablespoonful of flour; to the third part add enough red sugar to color it. Put it together with frosting.

Dolly Varden Cake.—One cup granulated sugar, one-half cup butter beaten to a cream, add one egg and the yolks of two more well beaten, one teaspoon of vanilla (or any essence you prefer), two-thirds cup sweet milk, one teaspoon baking powder, and flour to make good consistency for layer cake. Put one-third dough in one jelly tin, one-third in another and add spices and chopped raisins and citrons to remainder. Use this for middle layer, putting together with frosting made from whites of two eggs and half cup pulverized sugar.

Corn-Starch Cake.—Two cupfuls sugar, one cupful butter rubbed to a cream with sugar, one cupful sweet milk, two cupfuls flour, three eggs, whites and yolks beaten separately, one-half cupful corn-starch, two teaspoonfuls cream tartar sifted well through the flour, one teaspoonful soda dissolved in hot water. Sift the corn-starch with the flour and add the last thing. This makes a perfectly delicious cake and is a large loaf.

Apple Cake.—Cut into eighths five apples; take two cups of flour, one cup of water, half a cup of lard, one cup sugar. Mix together and roll out into dough, large enough to cover an ordinary baking pan. Grease the pan before putting in the dough, with the cut apples on top, and bake slowly for a-half hour.

Dried Apple Cake.—Soak one and one-half cups dried apples in as little water as possible over night. In the morning drain, chop and boil half an hour in one cup of syrup. Add, when the apples are slightly warm, one-half cup of butter and two-thirds cup of sugar beaten to a cream, then two well-beaten eggs, two heaping cups of flour, a teaspoon and a-half of yeast powder, one-half cup of raisins, small teaspoonful cloves, one cinnamon and one nutmeg, salt and lemon. Bake slowly in a moderate oven.

Pound Cake.—One pound of butter, one pound of sugar, one pound of flour, nine eggs, nutmeg to taste.

One Pound Cake.—One pound seedless raisins, one pound currants, one-half pound citron, one-half pound almonds, one pound coffee sugar, three-fourths pound butter, one pound flour, two teaspoonfuls cinnamon, one teaspoonful cloves, two teaspoonfuls allspice, one teaspoonful baking powder, vanilla to taste.

One, Two, Three, Four Cake.—One cup butter, one cup buttermilk, two cups sugar, three cups flour, four eggs, one teaspoon soda, two teaspoons cream tartar, lemon essence to taste.

Fruit Cake.—One-half cup of butter, one-half cup of brown sugar, one-half cup of molasses, one-half cup of sour milk, the yolks of four eggs, one-half teaspoon of soda, one teaspoon of cream tartar, one and one-half cups of flour one cup of raisins chopped fine, one cup of currants, one teaspoon each of cloves, cinnamon and nutmeg. The whites can be used for Delicate Cake.

Cheap Fruit Cake.—One cup of butter, one cup of sugar, one cup of molasses, four eggs, one-half pound chopped raisins, one-half pound currants, one-fourth pound citron, one-half teaspoonful cloves, cinnamon and nutmeg, one-half teaspoon soda, three and one-half teacups flour.

Fruit Cake—Two cups of sugar, one-half cup molasses, two eggs, one and one-half cups sour milk, one cup butter, one teaspoonful saleratus, one and one-half cups raisins, one cup currants.

White Fruit Cake.—Two cups of white sugar beaten to a cream, with one cup of butter, one cup of milk, two and one-half cups of flour, whites of seven eggs, two teaspoonfuls of baking powder. Mix thoroughly and add one pound each of sliced citron, raisins, blanched almonds and figs.

White Fruit Cake.—Two eggs, one-half cup butter, one-half cup sweet milk, one cup sugar, one cup raisins, two teaspoons baking powder.

Tumbler Fruit Cake.—One tumbler of butter, one tumbler of sugar, one tumbler of molasses, one tumbler of eggs, one pound of raisins, one pound of currants, one-half pound of citron, one-fourth teaspoonful of soda, one teaspoonful of all kinds of spice and salt.

Yellow Pound Cake.—One cup butter, two cups sugar, three cups flour, one-half cup sweet milk, yolk of six eggs and one whole one, one teaspoon cream tartar, one-half teaspoon soda, one-quarter pound citron, one cup raisins stoned.

Wedding Fruit Cake.—One pound butter, one pound sugar, eight eggs, one pound flour, one pound currants, one pound raisins, one-half pound citron, one ounce cinnamon, two nutmegs, one ounce cloves, one wineglassful brandy, three teaspoonfuls baking powder mixed in the flour.

Cup Cake.—Four cups flour, two cups sugar, one cup butter, one cup cream, one cup raisins, one cup currants, four eggs, one lemon, two teaspoons baking powder. Beat the butter and sugar to a cream. Stir in slowly a little flour, after it has been thoroughly mixed with the baking powder. Then pour in the cream, the raisins and currants, the beaten eggs, and the grated rind of one lemon. Stir in the rest of the flour. Bake in quick oven.

Cream Cake.—Break two eggs into a coffee cup, fill with cream, one cup white sugar, one and one-half cups flour, one teaspoon cream tartar, one-half teaspoon soda and a little lemon ; make it in the usual way ; very nice.

Gold Cake.—One and one-half cups sugar, one-half cup butter, one cup sweet milk, one teaspoonful cream tartar, one teaspoonful soda, nutmeg, three cups flour, yolks of six eggs.

Silver Cake.—One and one-half cups sugar, one-half cup butter, one cup sweet milk, one-half teaspoonful of soda, one teaspoonful of cream tartar, whites of six eggs beaten to a froth and three cups flour.

Mountain Cake.—Two eggs, two cups flour, one cup white sugar, one-half cup butter, one-half cup milk, one teaspoon cream tartar in the flour, one-half teaspoon saleratus in the milk. Flavor to taste. Two teaspoons of baking powder may be used in place of cream tartar and saleratus.

White Mountain Cake.—Two cups sugar, two eggs, one cup sweet milk, three and one-half cups flour, one-half cup butter, one teaspoonful soda, two teaspoonfuls cream tartar, and one teaspoonful lemon.

White Mountain Cake.—Two cups of sugar, one cup of butter, one cup of sweet milk, three cups of flour, four large eggs, one teaspoonful of cream tartar, one-half teaspoonful of saleratus.

Poor Man's Cake.—One cupful of cream, one of sugar, two of flour, one egg, one teaspoonful of soda and two of cream tartar.

Bridgeport Cake.—One cup of butter, two cups of sugar, four eggs, three and one-half cups of flour, one cup of milk, two cups of currants, one-half pound of citron, one teaspoon of saleratus, juice and grated rind of one lemon.

Delicious Cake.—Two cups of sugar, one cup of butter, three cups of flour, one cup of milk, four eggs, one teaspoonful of cream tartar, one-half teaspoonful soda, one teaspoonful of extract of lemon.

Buttermilk Cake.—One cup buttermilk, one cup molasses, one tablespoon shortening, spice to suit the taste, flour to make a thick batter. Bake slowly.

Plain Tea Cake.—Rub together four teaspoonfuls of butter, one cup of sugar, and one well-beaten egg, and one tablespoonful of cream, sift two teaspoonfuls of baking powder into two cups of flour. Bake in small pans and eat the cakes while they are fresh.

Pork Cake.—One cup each of chopped fat pork, raisins, sugar, molasses, hot water, one teaspoon each of cloves, cinnamon, nutmeg and soda ; stir rather thick.

Pork Cake.—One pound salt fat pork, chopped fine, one pound each of raisins and currants, one-fourth of citron or lemon peel, one cup brown sugar, one cup molasses, one teaspoon allspice, cinnamon and cloves, one teaspoon saleratus, one cup cold coffee or sour milk, six eggs, (is good without), enough flour to make stiff batter. Bake from two to three hours in a moderate oven.

Easter Cake.—One cup white sugar, one and one-half cups butter, two eggs, two small teaspoonfuls yeast powder, two cups flour. Lemon and salt. It would be well to bake a little of the batter to see that there is sufficient flour in the cake.

Dayton Cake.—Two cups of sugar, one cup of butter, four eggs, one cup of milk, one teaspoonful of soda, two teaspoonfuls of cream tartar, three cups flour. Flavor, mix cream tartar and soda in the flour.

Coffee Cake.—One cup cold coffee, one cup molasses, one cup sugar, one cup butter, three cups flour, one egg, one-half pound raisins, one-fourth pound citron, one tablespoon soda, one-half nutmeg, one teaspoon cinnamon, one-half teaspoon cloves. This makes two loaves. Bake slowly.

Coffee Cake.—One cup of brown sugar, one cup of molasses, one cup of butter, one cup of black coffee, five cups of flour, two eggs, one teaspoonful of soda, one teaspoonful each ground cinnamon, cloves, and nutmeg, one cup of raisins. This will make two cakes.

German Coffee Cake.—Two teacupfuls light dough bread, one teacupful of sugar, one-half teacupful of butter, one egg; mix well together, let it rise, then roll out upon the molding board place sheets in baking pans after ro ling not too thin; cover top of each cake with this mixture ; roll very fine one teacupful almonds, add one-half cupful cream, one-half cupful of sugar; when cakes are half baked spread this over the top of each. Bake very carefully.

Coffee Cake.—One cup of sugar, one cup of molasses, one cup of coffee, two-thirds of a cup of butter, two cups of chopped raisins two teaspoons soda, one teaspoon of all kinds of spice. Bake one hour in a moderate oven. This makes two loaves.

Spice Cake.—One cupful butter, two cupfuls sugar, one-half cupful milk, five eggs, three teaspoonfuls baking powder, one teaspoonful each of cinnamon, allspice, nutmeg, one-half cloves, flour to make quite stiff. This makes a large loaf, and will keep some time if wrapped in a cloth.

Ginger Cake (Excellent.)—One cup butter, two of sugar, four eggs, one cup milk, two teaspoonfuls ginger, three cups flour, two teaspoonfuls baking powder. Sift sugar over top before putting it in the oven.

Tumbler Cake.—One tumbler of molasses, one of sugar, one of eggs, one of butter, two of raisins, four of flour, two teaspoons of soda, one teaspoon of all kinds of spice. This makes two loaves. Bake one hour.

Mrs. Hasting's French Cake.—One-half cup butter, three eggs, two cups sugar, one cup milk, three cups flour, two teaspoons cream tartar and one teaspoonful soda. Beat the yolks of eggs in the milk, add butter and sugar, then flour and cream tartar, then the whites of eggs, and last of all the soda. Use no flavoring.

Watermelon Cake.—White part, two cups of white sugar, two-thirds cup of butter, two-thirds cup of milk, three cups of flour, whites of five eggs, one teaspoonful of soda, two teaspoonfuls of cream tartar. Red part, one cup of red sugar, one-half cup of butter, one-half cup of milk, two cups of flour, one cup of raisins, whites of five eggs, one teaspoonful of soda, and two teaspoonfuls of cream tartar. Stone and roll the raisins in powdered sugar, stir into the cake, and turn into the middle of the pan, and pour the white part over and around it.

Watermelon Cake.—One cup of white sugar and half a cup of butter, beaten to a cream; whites of three eggs beaten to a froth, half a cup of sweet milk, half a teaspoonful of soda dissolved in the milk; two cupfuls of flour, one teaspoonful of cream tartar in the flour; stir the whites of the eggs in last. Take a little more than one-third of the batter in another dish, add to it a teaspoonful of liquid cochineal, and a handful of seeded raisins; bake in a round loaf with the pink part in the centre of it. Make a frosting colored with green sand sugar or spinach. Flavor the cake with vanilla.

Surprise Cake.—One-half cup of butter creamed, one cup of sugar, a few drops extract of lemon or almond, one egg well beaten, one-half cup sweet milk, one-half teaspoonful soda, one teaspoon cream tartar, two cups of flour.

M. J. V. C.'s Spice Cake.—One cup sugar, one cup molasses, one cup sour milk, two-thirds cup shortening, three eggs, three large cups flour, one and one-half teaspoons soda, one of cloves, two of cinnamon, one of grated nutmeg, raisins or currants, many as you please.

Spice Cake.—One cup molasses, one cup sugar, two-thirds cup butter, one cup sour milk, three eggs, teaspoon soda, one nutmeg, one teaspoon cinnamon, one teaspoon cloves, three cups of flour.

Astonishment Cake.—One cup sugar, two cups flour, three eggs, three tablespoons cream, one teaspoon cream tartar, one-half teaspoon soda, spice to taste.

Pound Cake.—Three cups sugar, one cup butter, one cup sweet milk, four eggs, one teaspoon cream of tartar, one and one-half teaspoons soda, three and one-half cups flour.

Mrs. J. Richardson's A Cake.—One cup of sugar, half cup of butter, cream butter and sugar, two eggs, (beaten separately), half cup of milk, two cups of flour, one teaspoonful of cream tartar, half a teaspoonful of soda.

Good Plain Cake.—One cup of sugar, one-half cup of milk, one and one-half cups of flour, one egg, one heaping teaspoonful of butter, two teaspoonfuls of baking powder.

Snow Cake.—One cup of sugar, one-half cup of butter, one-half cup of milk, two cups of flour, whites of three eggs, one-half teaspoonful of soda, one teaspoonful cream tartar, sifted with the flour; beat butter and sugar together; add whites of eggs, beaten to a foam; flour, milk and soda last.   Flavor with nutmeg or lemon.   Use the yolks for frosting.

Delicate Cake.—The whites of four eggs well beaten, one cup of white sugar, one-half cup of butter, one-half cup of sweet milk, two cups of flour, one teaspoon cream tartar, one-half teaspoon of soda.

Silver Cake.—One cup sugar, one-half cup of shortening beat to a cream, then add one-half teaspoon of soda, dissolved in half cup of sweet milk, two cups of sifted flour, mixed with one teaspoon of cream tartar, season with nutmeg and lemon or vanilla. Now add the whites of two eggs beaten to a stiff froth.   Good and cheap.   For gold cake make the same as silver, using the yolks of the two eggs.

Snow Cake.—One-half cup butter, one cup sugar, two cups flour, whites of four eggs, one-half cup of sweet milk, one teaspoon baking powder, flavor with lemon.

Virginia's Snow Cake.—Two full cups of flour, one-half cup of milk, whites of four eggs, one-half cup of butter, one and one-half cups of sugar, one-half teaspoonful of soda, one teaspoonful of cream tartar; flavor with almond or lemon.

Lady Cake.—Three cups of flour, two cups of sugar, one cup of milk, one-half cup of butter, whites of four eggs; two teaspoonfuls of baking powder; add lemon extract.

White Cake.—One cup of butter, two cups sugar, one cup sweet milk, whites of five eggs, three cups of flour, two teaspoonfuls of baking powder, flavor to taste.

Angel Cake.—Whites of five eggs, one cup of sugar, small teaspoonful of cream tartar, one teaspoonful lemon. Beat this quantity to a stiff froth with a fork; one cup of flour after sifted. Bake in a quick oven fifteen minutes.

Sunshine Cake.—Whites of eleven eggs, yolk or six eggs, one and one-half cups of granulated sugar, measured after one sifting; one cup flour, measured after one sifting, one teaspoon of cream tartar, one teaspoon of extract of vanilla. Beat the whites to a stiff froth, and gradually beat in the sugar, beat yolks in a similar manner. Add the whites, sugar and flavor to the yolks, mix quickly and well, bake fifty minutes in a slow oven. Do not grease the pan.

Delicate Cake.—Whites of seven eggs, two cups white sugar, one cup butter, one cup sweet milk, three and one-half even cups flour, two teaspoons baking powder, lemon extract to taste.

Custard Cake.—Four eggs, four tablespoonfuls of water, one cup sugar, one and one-half cups flour, two heaping teaspoonfuls of baking powder. Bake in three layers. Filling: One cup sweet milk, butter size of an egg, two heaping tablespoonfuls of sugar, set this in boiling water and let it come to a boiling point; stir in one tablespoonful of corn starch, dissolved in cold water. When this thickens let it cool and add flavoring.

Cream Pie.—CAKE: Three eggs, one cup of sugar, one cup of flour, one teaspoonful of yeast powder or baking powder, and a teaspoonful of hot water the last thing. Beat the eggs and sugar to a cream, then add hot water and flour. Bake in three layers in a hot oven. CREAM FOR INSIDE: One pint of milk; put it on to boil, beat an egg with a tablespoonful of corn starch, and stir in; sweeten to taste; let it boil up thick; flavor with vanilla, and spread on the layers of cake.

Cream Cake.—One egg beaten separate, one cup sugar, five tablespoons melted butter, two-thirds cup of milk, two cups flour, three teaspoons baking powder, flavor with one tablespoon lemon Cream for cake: Put a cup and a-half sweet milk on to boil, take one egg, one-half cup sugar, two tablespoons flour, beat egg, sugar and flour well together, stir into the milk when boiling, flavor with a tablespoonful of lemon when done, let it boil till thick. Let the cake get cold before putting together, but have the cream hot.

Layer Cake.—Two cups flour, two large teaspoons baking powder, one egg, one cup sugar, small half cup butter, three-fourths cup sweet milk. For filling take thick sweet cream from one pan of milk, beat it until it becomes thick, sweeten and flavor with whatever suits the taste. Spread it between the layers when the cake is cold.

Jelly Roll.—Three eggs well beaten, one cup sugar, one and one-half cups flour, one teaspoon baking powder.

Jelly Cake.—Four eggs, two cups sugar, one scant cup butter, one cup milk, one small teaspoon soda, two small teaspoons cream tarter. Beat the whites and yolks separately. Beat the butter and sugar very light, then add the eggs and other ingredients, and stir in just enough flour to stiffen, about two cups. Bake in jelly cake tins. When cold, spread with currant or grape jelly and ice. Flavor with rind of one lemon.

Velvet Sponge Cake.—Two cups sugar, six eggs, leaving out the whites of three, one cup of boiling water, two and one-half cups flour, one teaspoon baking powder. Beat the yolks a little, add the sugar and beat fifteen minutes. Add the three beaten whites, and the cup of boiling water just before the flour. Flavor with a teaspoonful of lemon, and bake in three layers, putting them together with an icing made of the three beaten whites, with six dessert spoons of sugar to each egg. One teaspoon of lemon.

Sponge Cake. — One pound of sugar, one-half pound of

flour, ten eggs, yolks and whites beaten separately. Beat yolks and sugar together. Flavor to taste.

Sponge Cake.—One egg well beaten, one cup sugar, one tablespoonful of butter, nearly cup cold water, oneteaspoon baking powder, one cup flour, season to taste.

German Sponge Cake.—One heaping cup granulated sugar, seven eggs, beat together one-half hour, stir in heaping cup flour, slowly, flavor to taste.

Sponge Cake.—Two cups sugar, two cups flour, four eggs, two heaping teaspoons baking powder, and last stir in two-thirds cup boiling water and bake.

Sponge Cake.—Four eggs, one coffee cup white sugar, one coffee cup sifted flour, a little rose prepared as follows: Beat the whites to a very stiff froth with a little salt, cover and set in a cool place, while you beat the yolk to a cream, then add sugar and rose and beat to a froth, then whites, beat again, then flour, beating all thoroughly; bake in pound-cake tins, twelve in a set in a quick oven, but do not burn; very nice.

Sponge Cake.—One cup of sugar, one cup of flour, one-quarter cup of cold water, three eggs, beat yolks and sugar together, then put in water and stir in flour lightly; beat the whites to a stiff froth and stir in. Do not beat anything but yolks and sugar.

Sponge Cake.—Beat the whites of four eggs fifteen minutes; stir in one cup granulated sugar thoroughly; stir into this the beaten yolks lightly; one cup of flour after it is sifted; one teaspoon extract lemon.

Cream Cakes.—One-half cup butter, one cup cold water boiled together, add a cup flour, simmer a short time; when partly cool add three eggs, one at a time, without beating; drop on a pan a dessertspoonful. Bake thoroughly in a very hot oven, when cool fill with cream made as follows: Two cups milk, three-quarter cup sugar, two eggs, two small tablespoonfuls of flour. Flavor with lemon.

Cream Puffs.—One cup boiling water, one-half cup butter, boil together, and while boiling stir in one cup dry sifted flour. Take from stove and stir to a paste; when cool break in three eggs, unbeaten, and stir five minutes; then drop in spoonfuls on a buttered tin, and bake in a quick oven twenty-five minutes. The puffs must not touch each other in the pan. When the puffs are cold, fill with one-half pint of sweet cream, whipped to a stiff froth, sweetened and flavored to taste.

Berry Bake.—One pint of flour before sifted, one cup sugar, one cup milk, one large spoonful butter, two eggs, one pint blueberries, one teaspoonful saleratus, two teaspoonfuls cream tartar. Beat the sugar and butter together and then the two eggs; stir the milk with them; then the flour with the saleratus and cream tartar thoroughly mixed; turn into shallow pans about an inch deep; bake in a quick oven; to be eaten warm.

Blueberry Cake.—One cup of sugar, one-half cup of butter, three eggs, one cup of milk, four cups flour, one and one-half teaspoonfuls cream tartar, one teaspoonful soda; rub one pint of berries in the flour; bake in two tins.

Berry Cake.—One cup sugar, two-third cup butter, two eggs, one cup milk, one-half teaspoonful soda, one teaspoonful cream tartar, enough flour to hold berries, or as stiff as ordinary cake.

Feather Cake.—Take three cups sifted flour, one and one-half cups sugar, one cup sweet milk, two teaspoons baking powder and a little essence of lemon, one egg, two tablespoonfuls of butter ; beat the butter and sugar to a cream, then add the milk, the egg well beaten and the essence; mix with the above two cups of flour and lastly add the third into which the baking powder has been stirred, bake in jelly tins in quick oven, putting icing between and on top.

Feather Cake.—Beat to a cream a-half cup of butter; add two of sugar and beat well; add one cup of milk with one teaspoonful of soda in it; beat together; then add one cup of sifted flour with two teaspoonfuls of cream tartar rubbed in it, add next the beaten yolks of three eggs; beat the whites until stiff; add them and then two more cups of flour; beat well between each successive addition; butter two medium-sized tins, put in the batter and bake for a-half hour in a moderate oven.

Feather Cake.—Take two cups sugar, one-half cup butter, two-thirds of a cup milk, three cups flour, three eggs, and three teaspoonfuls Horsford's baking powder. Flavor with lemon or vanilla. This is a very nice plain cake.

Feather Cake.—One cup of white sugar, one teaspoonful of butter, one egg, two-thirds cup of milk, two even cups of flour, two even teaspoonfuls of cream tartar, one of soda, flavor with lemon. It is delicious.

Hurry Cake.—One cup sugar, one egg, half a cup cold water, butter size of an egg, and two teaspoons baking powder and one cup flour sifted together. Flavor to taste, nice for tea.

Tea Cake.—One cup of butter, two cups of sugar, three cups of flour, four eggs, (whites and yolks beaten separately), one cup sour milk, one teaspoonful soda, flavor with lemon. Mix the ingredients thoroughly together, and add whites of eggs, which have been previously beaten to a stiff froth.

Cream Sponge Cake.—Beat together a cupful of sugar and the yolks of three eggs, add a-half teaspoonful of soda, a teaspoon cream tartar, a cupful of flour and the whites of the eggs; bake in three layers and put between them the following: One egg, a-half cupful of cream, a cupful of sugar, a piece of butter the size of a walnut, boil until like cream, when cold season to taste.

Swiss Cake.—One quarter cup of butter, one and a-half cups of sugar, two and a-half cups of flour, one cup of sweet milk, two eggs, one teaspoonful of cream tartar, half teaspoonful of soda; stir the butter and sugar to a cream, and add the eggs last well beaten; flavor with lemon.

Cottage Cake.—One cup sugar, one tablespoon of butter, two eggs, one-half cup milk, one teaspoon cream tartar, one and one-half cups of flour, nutmeg or lemon; this is good baked in three shallow tins, with layers of chocolate or cocoanut and cream between the layers.

Eggless Cake.—One cup sugar, three tablespoonfuls butter, one cup sweet milk, two cups flour and two spoons baking powder; a very good cake when eggs are scarce and high.

PART VII.

Pies, etc.

Lemon Tarts.—Juice and rind of one lemon, one cup sugar and yolk of an egg, beat well and add one cup water in which is stirred a dessertspoonful corn-starch. Put over the fire and let come to a boil. Have some nice pastry shells and fill when cold. Frost with the white of the egg and sugar.

Brambles.—One cup raisins chopped fine, one cracker pounded fine, one lemon, grate the rind, chop the pulp; three-fourths cup of sugar, butter size of an egg. For the crust, two and one-half cups of flour, one egg, one-half cup lard. Roll thin, cut with a pint pail cover, wet the edges and put on a teaspoonful of the above mixture, fold over one-half and press the edges together, prick holes in the top.

Lemon Raisin Pie.—One cup chopped raisins, one lemon, one cup cold water, one tablespoonful flour, one cup sugar. Bake with upper and under crust.

Cream Pie.—Stir smooth two large teaspoonfuls of flour in a cup of new milk, add another cupful of very rich cream, three tablespoonfuls of sugar, a dash of salt and little flavoring. Bake with one crust.

Boiled Cider Pie.—One egg, one cup dry sugar, two tablespoons corn-starch, beaten together; half cup boiled cider, two-thirds cup cold water, one teaspoon extract lemon—this can be baked with two crusts, like a custard pie.

Raisin Pie.—One cup of raisins, stoned and chopped fine, one cup of hot water, juice of one lemon and grated rind, one cup of rolled crackers. Boil the raisins in just water enough to soften, add a pinch of salt and a cup of sugar, or half a cup sugar and half a cup of molasses.

Lemon Pie.—Put two large cups water in a basin, set it over a kettle of water on the stove. Take a nice lemon, grate it all, remove seeds and add the yolks of three eggs, two cups brown sugar, butter size of thumb, three tablespoons corn-starch mixed smooth in a little water, stir until thickened, and set away to cool. Now make a rich crust, put upon two pie tins and bake. Then fill with mixture: Beat whites of three eggs stiff and three tablespoons fine sugar, spread equally on two pies and brown slightly in oven.

Vinegar Pie.—One egg, one heaping tablespoon flour, one teacup sugar, beat all well together; add one tablespoon sharp vinegar, one teacup cold water, flavor with nutmeg; bake in two crusts.

Crumb Pie.—Soak in a little warm water, one teacup bread crumbs for half an hour; three tablespoons sugar, one-half table-spoon butter, one-half cup of cold water, a little vinegar, and nut-meg to suit the taste; bake with two crusts.

Mock Mince Pies.—One large cup powdered cracker, two cups sugar, one cup molasses, one cup vinegar, one cup chopped raisins, one cup warm water, one-half cup of butter, one teaspoon each of cinnamon, cloves, allspice, nutmeg, a little salt, a few drops of essence of lemon, two eggs. This will make two pies.

Lemon Custard.—Six eggs, beaten separately; one and one-half cups sugar, tablespoonful of butter, juice (only) of one large or two small lemons, mix the whites in last, bake immediately. For two custards, on puff paste.

Lemon Pie.—Two and one-half tablespoons of corn-starch, mix thoroughly in a little cold water, add a pint and one-half of boiling water, while this is partially cooling, prepare the juice and grated rind of two and one-half lemons, one and one-third cups of sugar and yolks of four eggs, mix well then pour in the corn-starch; line two pie-dishes with pastry, fill them with the mixture and bake half an hour, then beat the whites of the eggs to a stiff froth, add two spoonfuls of white sugar, spread over the pies and return to the oven to brown.

Potato Custard.—One quart of well-mashed sweet potatoes, three-fourths of a pound of butter, one and one-fourths pounds of sugar, six eggs, well beaten; flavor with lemon. Bake on puff paste.

Lemon Pie.—Put the yolks of three eggs in a bowl, add one teacupful of sugar, one teaspoon of butter, grate in the yellow rind of one lemon, (be careful to keep seeds out) squeeze out all the juice of lemon throwing away the white peel, add two table-spoons of flour and one half cup of milk or water, beat well, then put a rich crust on pie tin, then pour in this mixture and bake, when done beat the whites of three eggs stiff, with two table-spoons of sugar, put over top, brown slightly.

Vinegar Pie.—One cup of sugar, one cup of vinegar, (not too sour) and boil; then add the yolk of one egg and four table-spoonfuls of flour to the above. Then fill in a crust already baked. For frosting use the white of an egg and two tablespoonfuls of sugar, and return to the oven and brown lightly.

Imitation of a Lemon Pie.—One cup of chopped rhubarb, scalded, one and one-half cups of sugar, yolks of three eggs, fla-vor with lemon, bake with one crust; beat the whites of the eggs to a stiff froth with two tablespoonfuls of powdered sugar, spread over the pie; then brown.

Cream Pie—One pint of sweet milk, white of one egg and yolks of three; two tablespoonfuls of sugar, two of corn-starch; beat all together; let it cool and flavor. Make a rich crust and bake separate and fill; beat the whites of two eggs to a froth, spread over the top and set in the oven to brown.

Grandma's Fried Pie.—One cup sour milk, a very little shortening, one teaspoonful soda, and a little salt. Mix with flour to the consistency of biscuit dough. Roll into round cakes and fry in hot lard, turning over soon as browned. Have your ber-ries sugared and mashed. Put together same as shortcake. This is excellent with cranberries and splendid with any kind of fruit. This will make four layers.

Prune Pie.—three cups prunes, one cup sugar, one teaspoon-ful extract of lemon, two tablespoonfuls vinegar. Stew, seed and mash prunes; add sugar, lemon, and vinegar. Have mixture rather juicy and bake with two crusts.

Sweet Apple Pie.—One and one-half large sweet apples, grated, one egg, one cup of sweet cream, milk to fill pie plate. Bake in one crust.

Banana Custard Pie.—Take two bananas, rub through a colander and have them perfectly smooth; mix the bananas with one pint of milk, two tablespoons of sugar, two eggs and a little salt. Bake in a medium sized plate in a slow oven.

Mince Pie.—One quart meat, one pint suet, two quarts of apples, one pint of sugar, one quart of raisins, one pint of molasses, boiled, two large spoonfuls cinnamon, one spoonful cloves, two nutmeg, teaspoonful of allspice, pint boiled cider, butter and salt to taste.

Lemon Meringue Pie.—One tablespoon of corn-starch, one cupful of boiling water, one cupful of sugar, piece of butter size of nutmeg, one lemon, two eggs. Wet the starch with cold water, and rub smooth. Stir it into the cup of boiling water on the stove. Let it boil up once, and then pour upon the butter and sugar. Stir well. When cold add the juice and grated rind of the lemon. Beat the eggs, reserving the white of one, and mix them in. Pour into a pie plate, lined with crust. Bake in a moderate oven for twenty minutes. When cool cover with a frosting made of white of egg reserved, and brown delicately.

Date Pie.—One pound of dates, one quart of milk and three eggs. Season the same as for squash pie. It needs no sweetening. Put the dates in the milk and heat until they are soft enough to sift. This makes two good-sized pies. Use one crust, the same as for squash.

Rhubarb Pie.—One and one-half teacups rhubarb cut fine, pour boiling water over and turn off; one-half teacup raisins cut in two, three-fourths teacup granulated sugar. Mix all together, sprinkle with flour, beat one egg and spread over top, put on upper crust and bake.

Mock Mince Pies with Bread Crumbs.—Bread crumbs, sugar, molasses, vinegar, boiling water, raisins and currants, each one cup; butter, one-half cup; spices to taste.

Lemon Pie.—One lemon, yolks of three eggs, one cup sugar, two tablespoons flour, one pint sweet milk, save whites for frosting.

Molasses Pie.—One pint molasses, one-half pint thick milk, one teacup lard or butter, three tablespoons flour, half teaspoon soda, one tablespoon of cinnamon. Will make four or five pies. Cover with strips.

Virginia Lemon Pie.—Squeeze the juice of two lemons on four tablespoonfuls of sugar, add one tablespoonful of butter, two eggs, and beat all together thoroughly, then add one small glass of milk and one teaspoonful of flour, beat the flour smoothly with a little of the milk; pour this in a crust being just sufficient for one pie. Bake about twenty minutes.

Sugar Pie.—Two cups sugar, one-half cup butter, one-half cup cream, three eggs, flavor with lemon extract, bake.

Lemcn Pie.—One lemon, one egg, one cup of sugar, bake with two crusts.

Buttermilk Pie.—Buttermilk just churned one and one-half cups, one cup of sugar, one teaspoon of melted butter, one tablespoon of flour, one egg, mix the flour in a little of the buttermilk. Bake in a quick oven, flavor with nutmeg.

Mock Mince Pie.—One cup bread crumbs, one cup molasses, one cup sugar, one cup vinegar, one cup water, one-half cup butter, raisins and spices to taste. This makes three pies.

Cream Pie.—Two eggs, three-quarters of a cup of sugar, one cup of flour, one-quarter of a cup of cold water, one heaping teaspoonful of baking powder, beat the eggs light, add sugar, water, flour and baking powder, sift flour before measuring; bake in one tin, split and put in cream. CREAM:—One-half pint of milk, one-half cup of sugar, one-fourth cup of flour, one-egg, pinch of salt, one teaspoon of vanilla; break egg on flour and sugar and mash, then stir into boiling milk until thick.

PART VIII.

Doughnuts, Cookies, Gingerbreads, etc.

Doughnuts.—One cup of sugar, two eggs, one cup of milk, one teaspoonful of soda, two teaspoonfuls cream tartar, one-half teaspoonful of butter. Sift the soda and cream tartar into the flour.

Plain Doughnuts.—One cup sugar, one egg, one pint sweet milk, two teaspoons cream tartar, one of soda, three tablespoons of sour cream.

Doughnuts.—One quart of flour, one cup of sugar, one cup sour milk, one egg, one teaspoonful of saleratus, and a pinch of salt, fry in hot lard.

Fannie's Doughnuts.—One cupful of sugar, two eggs, beaten thoroughly, a cupful of sweet milk, two teaspoonfuls of cream tartar sifted through the flour, a teaspoonful of soda dissolved in the milk, a teaspoonful of salt, a little nutmeg and cinnamon; flour enough just to handle, roll out, cut with a doughnut cutter, and fry a nice brown in hot lard.

Delicious Doughnuts.—Take one quart of flour, one cup of sugar, one cup of sweet milk, one egg, a pinch of salt, one teaspoonful of saleratus, and two of cream tartar. Fry in lard.

Crullers.—One egg, one cup of sugar, one cup of sour cream, one small teaspoonful of soda, one small pinch of salt, spice with nutmeg to suit the taste, mix soft, roll nearly an inch thick, cut out with a cake cutter that has a hole in the centre. Fry in hot lard.

Excellent Doughnuts.—Three well beaten eggs, one teacup sugar, one teacup cream, nutmeg as desired, one teacup new milk, one teaspoonful salt and one of soda in the new milk, flour to mould soft.

Cocoanut Jumbles.—One cup of butter, two cups of sugar, two eggs, one large cup grated cocoanut. Use flour enough to make a dough that can be rolled. Bake the cakes in a quick oven.

Jumbles.—One-half cup of butter, one cup of sugar, two eggs, and one-fourth teaspoonful of soda, roll thin and sprinkle sugar over them.

Rich Jumbles.—One pound butter, one pound sugar, one and one-half pounds flour, four eggs, roll in powdered sugar and bake. These are good to keep a long time and be nice.

Drop Cakes.—Four eggs, well beaten separately, one cup of sugar, one-half cup of butter, one cup of corn-starch, two teaspoons of baking powder, bake in tins same as the above recipe, place a large raisin in the top of each one after they are put in the tins.

Almond Cakes.—Into one pound of flour, rub six ounces of butter, add salt, one-half pound sugar, ten drops of essence of almond. Whisk three eggs and mix with the ingredients into a stiff paste. Roll and cut into cakes with a tin cutter and bake slowly. Keep in a tin canister.

Fruit Cookies.—One and one-half cups sugar, one-half cup butter, two eggs, one and one-half cups chopped raisins, one-quarter cup currants, one-half teaspoon cinnamon, cloves and allspice, one teaspoon nutmeg, one-half cup milk, flour to roll. Cut in thin cakes.

Raisin Cookies.—Two eggs, one cupful of sugar, one half cupful of butter, one cupful chopped raisins, one-half cupful of milk, one teaspoonful cream tartar, one half teaspoonful of soda, spice.

Fruit Cookies—Two cups of sugar, one and one-third cups of butter, three eggs, one cup of chopped raisins, one cup of currants, one teaspoonful each of cloves, cassia and soda, one nutmeg, flour to make quite stiff.

Cocoanut Cookies.—One cupful of butter, two cupfuls of sugar, two cupsfuls prepared or grated cocoanut, two eggs, flour enough to make a stiff batter, and one teaspoonful of soda; drop on buttered paper in tin pans.

Cinnamon Drops.—One egg, one cup of sugar, one cup of molasses, one-half cup of butter, one cup of water, two teaspoonfuls of cinnamon, heaping teaspoonful of soda, five small cups of flour, bake in "patty pans."

Eggless Cookies.—Two cups sugar, one of sweet milk, one teaspoon soda, one cup of butter or shortening. This recipe will be found convenient when eggs and cream are scarce. Season with nutmeg.

Cream Cookies.—One cup rich sour cream, one tablespoonful butter, one cup sugar, one-half teaspoonful salt, one-half teaspoonful soda, flavor with nutmeg.

Cream Cookies.—One cup of sour milk, one of sugar, one-third teaspoon of soda, a pinch of salt, nutmeg, flour, stir the cream, sugar, soda together, and then the flour, make soft, bake quickly.

Cookies.—One teacup sugar, one egg, one-half cup butter, nutmeg for spice, one even teaspoon of soda dissolved in two spoonfuls of sweet milk, flour to mould.

Farmer's Cookies.—One cup white sugar, one egg, one cup good, thick, sour cream, one-half teaspoonful salt, one teaspoon saleratus, mix with dough quite stiff.

Sugar Cookies.—Two cups of sugar, one cup of butter, two eggs, one teaspoonful of soda, two teaspoonfuls of cream tartar, one-fourth of a cup of water, one-half of a grated nutmeg, and flour to thicken.

Cookies.—Two cups sugar, one cup butter mixed with sugar with the hand thoroughly, two tablespoonfuls of milk, three teaspoons baking powder, flavor with lemon or nutmeg, flour to roll out.

Cookies.—Two eggs, three cups white sugar, rolled fine and well beaten together, two cups lard, one cup sour milk, two teaspoonfuls soda.

Cookies.—Two eggs, one cup sugar, one-half cup butter, one-half teaspoonful soda dissolved in a teaspoonful of milk, one teaspoonful cream tartar and flour to roll out. Flavor to taste.

Cookies.—Two cups sugar, one cup butter, or meat fryings, one cup buttermilk, teaspoonful soda, cream the butter and sugar together first, then add milk, soda and flour to roll, do not knead but mix thoroughly before taking on the board, flavor to taste, use nutmeg, two teaspoons of lemon extract, roll thin, bake in quick oven.

Hickory Nut Cake.—One egg, one half cup flour, one cup sugar, one cup nuts sliced fine, drop on buttered tins two inches apart.

Soft Gingerbread.—One cup of molasses, half cup of milk, one-third cup butter, one teaspoon ginger, three and one-half cups flour, one teaspoon soda dissolved in the milk.

Soft Gingerbread.—One cup molasses, one cup boiling hot water, one tablespoon lard, one of ginger, one teaspoon soda, mix very soft, and add one egg. Bake quick.

Soft Gingerbread.—One cup of molasses, one cup of water, two and one-half cups flour, one teaspoon soda in water, three tablespoons melted butter, ginger and allspice to taste.

Hard Gingerbread.—One cup butter, two of sugar, one egg, one cup milk, teaspoonful ginger, two of baking powder, flour to roll out.

Drop Ginger Cookies.—One cup molasses, one cup sour cream, one-half cup sugar, one egg, one teaspoon soda, one teaspoon ginger, one teaspoon cinnamon.

Ginger Cookies.—Two eggs, one cup molasses, one-half cup sugar, one cup butter or lard, two teaspoonfuls soda, dissolved in one-fourth cup of cold water, one teaspoonful ginger, flour to mix soft.

Ginger Cookies.—One cup of sugar, two cups of molases, one cup of lard, two-thirds cup of sour milk, two eggs, one teaspoon ginger, one teaspoon cinnamon, one teaspoon cloves, one teaspoon soda, one tablespoon salt, flour enough to roll.

Excellent Ginger Snaps.—Two cups of molasses, one cup lard, one teaspoon soda, salt and ginger, flour to stiffen, roll thin and bake quickly.

Ginger Snaps.—One cup molasses, one cup sugar, one scant cup lard, one egg, tablespoon ginger, one teaspoon soda.

Ginger Snaps.—Two-thirds cup butter, one cup molasses, one cup sugar, one heaping teaspoonful ginger, one ¦of cloves, one of soda, dissolved in hot water. Flour to mould. Bake quick.

Ginger Snaps.—One cup molasses, heated, one-half cup

sugar, one egg, one tablespoon ginger, one tablespoon soda, three tablespoons vinegar, one-half teaspoon salt.

Sallie's Ginger Snaps.—One coffee cup each of lard, molasses and sugar, three teaspoonfuls of vinegar, six teaspoonfuls of water, one heaping teaspoonful of soda, one teaspoonful of ginger or cinnamon, flour to roll easily. Roll very thin.

Ginger Snaps.—One pint molasses, one cup shortening, (drippings, lard or butter, if plenty,) one teaspoonful of soda, one teaspoonful of ginger. Boil up thoroughly, mix stiff while warm, not hot, roll thin and bake quickly.

Springfield Rumville Snaps.—Three-fourths cupful lard, three-fourths cupful butter, one cupful sugar, one pint molasses, one teaspoonful soda, one tablespoonful ginger, one tablespoonful spice, then enough flour to roll soft and very thin in rings.

Ginger Drops.—One cup brown sugar, one cup molasses, one-half cup butter, two eggs, one teaspoon cinnamon, one teaspoon ginger, two teaspoons soda, stir stiff. This makes about forty drops.

Ginger Snaps.—One cup molasses, one-half cup sugar, one cup butter, and lard mixed, one teaspoon soda, dissolved in water, one teaspoon ginger and cinnamon each, boil all together and when cool, stir in flour enough to mould and bake.

PART IX.

Frostings and Sauces.

'**Berry Sauce (for Puddings.)**—One and one-half teaspoon-fuls corn-starch, wet in a little cold water. Pour over it one pint of boiling water, add one cup of sugar, and butter size of a nutmeg, boil till it begins to thicken then pour over a pint of chopped berries.

Pudding Sauce.—Beat the white of one egg stiff, the yolk to a cream; mix with one cup of sugar, add boiling water till the sauce is as thick as custard ; flavor with lemon.

Excellent Pudding Sauce.—Beat the white of an egg to a stiff froth, the yolk to a cream, and mixing it with one cup of pulverized sugar. Add boiling water till the sauce is of the consistency of boiled custard. Flavor with lemon, rosewater or vanilla, or with any other extract.

Sauce for Pudding.—A half-cup of sugar rolled till fine and beaten to a cream with half a cup of butter is very good; with vanilla, it is better. Plain cream, taken from sweet milk, is excellent.

Pudding Sauce.—Delicious pudding sauce is made of mixed fruits, chopped fine and cooked until soft. Thin properly with water and sweeten, and lastly add a well-beaten egg. Serve hot or cold.

Wine Sauce.—Beat a cupful of butter till it is creamy; then gradually beat into it two cupfuls of powdered sugar, and when this is done, add a gill of sherry by spoonfuls. Beat the mixture until it becomes a smooth, light froth; then set the bowl in a basin of boiling water and stir for a minute and a-half. Have the sauce bowl or boat heated by means of boiling water. When the sauce is finished, empty the bowl of water and put the sauce into it. Grate a part of a nutmeg over the sauce and send to the table hot.

Pudding Sauce.—A tablespoonful of corn-starch wet up evenly in a little cold water and stirred into a pint of boiling water and a-half cup of molasses is nice. A different flavor can be given by adding the juice of a lemon or a tablespoonful of vinegar.

A Rich Sauce.—Rub one small cup of butter, and two of sugar, to a cream, then stir in three eggs, beaten very light, and two tablespoonfuls of boiling water, and flavor with lemon or wine.

Pudding Sauce for Steam Pudding.—One cupful of brown sugar, one-half cupful butter, or if less is used, a pinch of salt, one dessertspoonful corn-starch, one-half teaspoonful cinnamon, less of cloves and a little nutmeg, stir all together thoroughly, pour on boiling water, stirring all the time until the sauce is as thick as desired.

Pudding Sauce.—One-half cup butter, two-thirds cup sugar, three spoons flour thoroughly mixed, add slowly, so as not to get it lumpy, enough boiling water to make it the thickness of good thick cream. Boil long enough to cook flour, add nutmeg and a spoonful of vinegar.

Recipe for Sauce.—One cup of water, one cup of white sugar, one tablespoonful of butter, one tablespoonful of vinegar, one tablespoonful of flour, a little salt, flavor with essence of lemon. Mix all well together except water; when beaten pour the water on boiling hot, and let the whole come to a boil.

Sauce for Pudding.—One cup butter, two cups sugar beaten to a cream, two eggs well beaten, put in a bowl and steam one hour. Just before using add one cup boiling water, one cup raspberry vinegar.

Salad Dressing.—One egg, two tablespoons sugar, one-half cup vinegar, butter size of half an egg, one teaspoon mustard, one-half teaspoon salt. Mix mustard, salt, sugar and vinegar, and pour on beaten egg. simmer all ten minutes, stirring all the time.

Salad Dressing.—One egg beaten, one-half teaspoonful each of mustard, salt and sugar, one-fourth teaspoonful of pepper, one-half a cup of vinegar, two tablespoonfuls of cream or butter. Set over boiling water to thicken.

Mayonnaise Sauce.—Two eggs, one-half teaspoon raw mustard, scarcely blended with vinegar. Mix with oil, drop by drop, thoroughly. Use plenty of oil, till the mixture is hard enough to be cut with a knife. Add yolks of two eggs stiffly beaten. Mix all together, and add half a teaspoon of salt, and the juice of one lemon. Place on ice till ready for use.

Egg Sauce.—Stir one ounce of butter and flour together over the fire till they bubble. Gradually add half a pint of boiling water, stirring the sauce with an egg-whip until smooh. Season with pepper, salt and a little chopped parsley, and juice of one lemon. Chop the yolk of hard boiled egg and put in the sauce just before using.

Mint Sauce is an improvement to a roast of mutton or lamb. Take the youngest leaves of the spearmint, cut away all the stems, chop very fine, put a teaspoonful of sugar to two or three of the mint, and use sufficient vinegar to be thoroughly flavored by the mint. Make at least an hour before it is to be used.

Caper Sauce.—Mix together two large tablespoonfuls of butter and one tablespoonful of flour; put into a saucepan with two cups water; set on the fire, cook till it thickens, then add capers to taste and salt. Take from the fire and add the yolk of an egg beaten. This sauce can be varied by using chopped cucumbers, hard boiled eggs or mushrooms.

Onion Sauce.—Boil one cup of milk, add a small piece of butter and a tablespoonful of flour, salt and pepper. When thick pour over three onions boiled and chopped fine.

French Dressing.—Two tablespoonfuls of sweet oil, one tablespoonful vinegar, saltspoonful of red pepper and half a teaspoonful of salt, all mixed together thoroughly.

Chocolate Icing.—Boil one and a-half cupfuls of sugar with three tablespoonfuls of cream, and a half a cake of chocolate, grated, then pour this over the beaten whites of two eggs, add a teaspoonful of vanilla, beat until it thickens.

Caramel Frosting.—Boil two minutes one cup sugar, one-half cup milk, flavor and beat to a cream. When nearly cool, spread over the cake, then spread on a layer of melted chocolate.

Cheap Frosting.—One even teaspoonful of gelatine, one even teaspoonful of cold water, soak one-half hour, add one tablespoonful of hot water, and one cup of pulverized sugar.

Cooked Icing.—One pound of granulated sugar, one-half tumbler of water, whites of three eggs. Boil sugar and water together, until it drops like candy from spoon, then pour hot over the eggs, beating rapidly.

Icing.—Four tablespoonfuls of water, juice of half a lemon, sufficient sugar to make a stiff paste. Spread all over the cake. It will harden in a short time.

To Color Icing.—Lemon juice will whiten frosting, while cranberry or strawberry will color it pink, and the grated rind of an orange strained through a cloth will color it yellow.

Chocolate Frosting.—Beat the whites of three eggs to a stiff froth, gradually add three cups of white sugar, beat very hard and add grated chocolate to suit taste. This is excellent for layer cake.

White Frosting.—The white of one egg, and five table-spoonfuls of powdered sugar. Break the whites of two eggs into a bowl, without beating, and one tablespoonful of corn-starch, and pulverized sugar enough to make it quite stiff, it will dry in a few minutes.

Chocolate Frosting.—One cup white sugar, enough water to moisten good, boil till a drop hangs like a thread from the spoon and snaps. Have ready one egg, beaten stiff; pour boiling syrup over egg and stir in grated chocolate about two tablespoonfuls; put on the top of cake while hot.

Fig Paste for Cake Filling.—Wash and chop fine one pound figs, then put with a cup each of sugar and water and cook till you have a thick paste; spread between the layers of cake.

Caramel Frosting.—One cup brown sugar, one square Baker's chocolate, scraped fine, one tablespoonful water. Simmer twenty minutes; spread on cake while hot.

Milk Frosting.—One cup white sugar, five tablespoons of sweet milk; boil together four or five minutes; stir hard until cold and spread on cold cake.

Chocolate Icing.—One cup sugar, yolk of four eggs, one-fourth cup milk, one-third cake chocolate. Mix all together and boil; when cool add a teaspoon vanilla and spread between layers.

PART X.

Pickles, Preserves and Confectionery.

Winter Chili Sauce.—One quart can tomatoes, six large onions; cook the onions until tender, pour in tomatoes, three teaspoonsful salt, two of cloves and allspice, and pepper, four cups vinegar, one and one-half cups sugar.

Conserves Peaches.—Weigh the fruit to one pound, use one-fourth pound sugar, steam fruit one-fourth hour until you can pierce with a straw, the fruit makes its own juice, put on dishes, cover with syrup, set in sun to dry, in a day or two turn each piece over, when half dry put on clean dishes with the rest of syrup and roll in granulated sugar and put in glass jars.

Damsons.—Put the fruit in stone jars, set in hot water to steam; when soft and pulpy pap through a sieve. To one pound of fruit use one-fourth pound sugar. Stew till thick, pour on dishes not too thick; when nearly dry cut in squares, roll in granulated sugar.

Cherries.—Stone the fruit and scald, using one-fourth pound sugar to one pound fruit; then proceed as in peaches.

Raspberries.—Wash, weigh, stew as damsons, put on dishes when nearly dry, cut in squares as for damsons. Any or all fruit done in this way equals the French conserves.

Blackberry Jelly.—Boil the berries till soft, and strain. To one pint of juice add one pint of granulated sugar, and boil together fifteen to twenty minutes.

Preserved Watermelon Rind or Citron.—Having pared and cut the rind, to each pound allow one and one-half pounds white sugar, and one pint of water. Heat the syrup sufficiently to strain easily, return to kettle and put in the rind, after having been in salt water, that will bear an egg, for three days, then in fresh water all night to remove the salt taste. Boil rapidly till nearly done, then more moderately till clear entirely through. If the rind is boiled in water without the sugar, it will not be clear and sweet all through. No need of alum water, ginger tea, vines, leaves, etc., only use lemon, vanilla, strawberry, any one flavoring you like best.

Currant Jelly.—Put your fruit into a stone jar, which must be placed in a pot of hot water, and keep it boiling until your currants are easily squeezed. This method gives less trouble and obtains more juice. Measure one pound of sugar to every pint of juice and put upon the fire; let it boil for twenty minutes. Don't paste up while hot.

Prune Jelly.—Stew two quarts of prunes slowly until very soft. Strain through a colander and save the prunes. Put the juice in a kettle and add half a package of gelatine which has been dissolved in cold water and a large cupful of sugar, boil fast twenty minutes and pour in tumblers. The prunes can be used for sauce, by adding a cup of sugar and a little water, and cooking as usual.

Stewed Pears.—Put them, well mashed, into a tight vessel, with sugar enough to sweeten, and water to keep from burning, a little stick cinnamon, or two or three whole cloves. Stew a long time.

Baked Pears.—Prepare as for stewing, but add no spice; set your dish in the oven and let it bake till the pears are dark and in a rich syrup.

Peaches.—Soft peaches preserved with the skins on are splendid. Open any freestone peaches you may happen to have, weigh them, and allow nearly one pound of white sugar to each pound of fruit. Place in a dish a layer of peaches and one of sugar, alternately, let stand over night, and in the morning boil in their own syrup till done. Peaches done in this way keep nicely.

Pumpkin Preserves.—Take a good round ripe pumpkin, peel and cut in inch squares, let stand over night in a weak solution of alum water, and in the morning spread on platters, set in the sun or in the oven for two hours, take three-fourths pound of sugar to a pound of pumpkin, one cup raisins and a lemon, cook till pumpkin is done, then skim out and cook juice until thick enough to keep as any other preserves, if made right can't be told from citron.

Gooseberry Jam.—To every pound of gooseberries add a pound of sugar. Bruise the gooseberries well in a mortar or kettle and boil them well. When cold put the jam in pots and seal over.

Tomato Honey.—Take six peach tree leaves to each pound of tomatoes, add a little water, and boil tender, strain off and weigh the juice, add one pound of sugar and one-half lemon to each pound of juice. Boil till thick as good molasses and put away for use. Does not have to be sealed.

Grape Jelly.—Pick the grapes, either green or ripe, from the stem; wash and drain them and mash them with a spoon. Put them in your preserving kettle and cover them with a plate. Boil ten minutes, then pour them into your jelly bag and squeeze out the juice. Put back into the kettle, with one pound of sugar to every pint of juice, and boil again for twenty minutes, skimming well.

Wild Grape Jelly.—Stew wild grapes until soft, then press through a flannel jelly bag. Boil juice twenty-five minutes, if a bright, clear day, if rainy or cloudy it will take fifteen minutes longer, then add sugar at the rate of one teacupful of sugar to four teacupfuls of juice, and boil until it jellies, when dropped on a cold plate. Place in jelly glasses, and keep in a dry, cool cellar.

Preserved Oranges.—Boil the oranges in clear water until you can pass a straw through their skins; then clarify three-quarters of a pound of sugar to a pound of fruit, and pour over the oranges while hot. Let them stand one night, then boil them in the syrup until they are clear and the syrup thick. Take them from the syrup, and strain it clear over them.

Preserved Citron.—Prepare the rind in any form desired, boil very hard in tolerably strong alum water for thirty or forty minutes, then take out and put into clear, cold water to stand over night; in the morning change the water and put on to boil, let cook until the citron has entirely changed color and is quite soft; then make a syrup, allowing one and one-half pounds of white sugar to one pound of fruit, put in the fruit, which needs but little more cooking; mace, ginger or lemon flavors nicely.

Canned Rhubarb.—Take fresh, tender stalks, pare them, cut into pieces about an inch long. Pack these pieces solidly in preserving jars. Fill the jars with cold water and let them stand over night. In the morning pour off all the water and fill the jars with fresh cold water. Put on the rubber bands, being careful that they fit perfectly. Now place the jars one at a time, under a stream of cold water and keep them there until the water overflows. Put on the cover, and seal while the water is still flowing over the jar. When all the jars have been sealed, wipe them and tighten the covers.

Ground Cherry Preserves. — Ground cherries or golden husk tomatoes, as they are sometimes called, make a very fine preserve. Select ripe fruit, make a syrup by dissolving in a little water one-half pound of sugar for each pound of fruit; when the cherries are cooked, remove with a perforated skimmer, boil syrup one-half hour, then pour over the fruit.

Apple Ginger. — Four pounds apples, four pounds light brown sugar, three lemons, one ounce white ginger root. Pare and chop apples fine; use the juice and grated rind of the lemons; get the ginger root in root form (it is fresher when procured at a druggist's); cook all together slowly three or four hours, or until it looks light and clear. This is delicious, and will keep for years as well as foreign sweetmeats. A little ginger root will give common apple sauce a most delicious flavor.

Apple Sauce.—Stew slowly, with a little water, three quarts of apples till soft; then add one teaspoon of salt, one full coffee cup of sugar, a piece of butter the size of an egg, and the grated rind and juice of two lemons. Stir well, cover and stew slowly a long time, till of a deep red color.

Lemon Taffy.—One cup of granulated sugar, one-fourth cup of water, and a pinch of cream tartar. Boil until it hardens when dropped in water; pour on buttered, pans and when cool enough so that it will not burn the hands pull until it is a silvery white. Twist in a rope and cut with a sharp shears.

Horehound Candy.— Three cups granulated sugar, one cup water. Boil until very brittle. Boil a spoonful of horehound in a little water; strain into the sugar while cooking. Pour on greased pan or marble, and cut in squares or sticks.

Lemon Drops.—Sugar and water same as for horehound. Pour out on well-greased tin or marble. Spread over the candy while hot one small tablespoonful of powdered citric acid, one teaspoonful oil of lemon; work until absorbed, flatten, cut in small pieces, with thimble or as you like.

Cocoanut Candy.—Three cups granulated or pulverized sugar, one cup water, pinch of cream tartar, boil from ten to fifteen minutes; when nearly done add one cup of cocoanut. Set the dish in a pan of cold water, and stir until it begins to thicken; pour on buttered plates to dry; an earthen dish is best; tin will do if new and bright.

Cocoanut Candy.—Grate the meat of a cocoanut and mix with it two pounds of sifted white sugar, the beaten whites of two eggs, and the milk of the nut. Make into little cakes, and in a short time it will be ready for use.

Honey Candy.—Two cups white sugar, one cup water, four tablespoonfuls of honey, boil until brittle on being dropped into water. Pull when cooling, and eat in any shape.

Ice Cream Candy.—One cup sugar, one-third cup of water, one-fourth teaspoonful of cream tartar, butter the size of an egg. Boil all together about fifteen minutes, not stirring till taken from the fire, when the extract is added.

Molasses Candy.—One cup of molasses, one-half cup of sugar, one teaspoonful of vinegar, butter two-thirds as large as a nutmeg. When boiled stir in a little soda.

Molasses Candy.—Three cups of sugar, one of water, pinch of cream tartar, butter one-half size of an egg. Flavor, pour on greased plates; pull on hook or with hands, and cut in any shape you wish.

Peppermints.—Two cups of sugar, one cup of water. Boil five minutes, then flavor with one spoonful of peppermint. Stir until thick, then drop.

Taffy.—Take a cup of good molasses, cup of granulated sugar, cup of sweet milk, butter the size of half an egg, then place them in a large spider over the fire, and stir constantly until hard; try some in a little cold water, and just before taking it from the fire add a quautity of English walnuts or shagbarks, or, if preferred, a little grated chocolate.

Cocoanut Drops.—To one cup of cocoanut add one-half cup of confectionery sugar and the white of one egg cut to a stiff froth, mix thoroughly and drop on buttered white paper. Bake fifteen minutes.

Chocolate Cream.—Two cups sugar, one-half cup cream and milk, small piece of butter; boil four minutes, set in cold water and stir until can mould; dip them in melted chocolate, butter and sugar.

Chocolate Creams.—Two and a-half cups granulated sugar, one-half cup cold water, boil four minutes in tin sauce-pan, set pan in dish cold water; stir till it creams, make into little balls; cut one-half cake Baker chocolate into bits, melt in a bowl set in hot water, stick a knitting needle in each cream ball, dip in chocolate; this makes eighty; lay on buttered paper.

Chocolate Creams.—One cup of sugar, one-half cup of water, one-half teaspoonful corn-starch. Boil about eight minutes and stir to a cream. Mould into little balls, place on paper, and, when cool, dip in dissolved chocolate.

Horehound Candy.—Boil two ounces dried horehound in one and one-half pints of water for half an hour, strain and add three and one-half pounds brown sugar, boil over a hot fire until sufficiently hard, pour out in flat well-greased tins, and mark in squares or sticks as soon as cool enough to retain its shape.

Chocolate Caramels.—Boil together for twenty minutes, one cup each of molasses, sugar, chocolate, sweet cream or milk, and a piece of butter size of an egg. Flavor with vanilla; try in water, stir a few minutes, pour out, cut in squares before cold.

Chocolate Caramels.—One teaspoonful of butter, two table-spoonfuls of grated chocolate dissolved in a little hot water, one large cup of granulated sugar, one half teaspoonful of cream tartar, and enough water to dissolve the sugar. Boil until it is brittle when dropped in water, pour on buttered pans, when cool cut it into squares and break apart when cold. Vanilla caramels are made in the same way by omitting the chocolate and substituting one tablespoonful of extract of vanilla.

Cream Candy.—This is made without cooking; the white of one egg, teaspoonful of sweet cream; stir in sugar enough so you can handle it with the hands, then make it in any shape you wish, cut with a thimble or make in balls, or in the shape of chocolate drops, and when cold dip in melted chocolate and lay on greased plates to dry. Season the ones to be made into chocolate drops or to cocoanuts, with vanilla; it can also be flavored with cinnamon, rose, peppermint, wintergreen, etc.

Cocoanut Drops.—One pound of cocoanut, one pound of powdered sugar, scant one-fourth pound of flour, whites of six eggs. Bake in a quick oven.

Cream Walnuts.—Crack English walnuts carefully, so as to take the meats out whole. Take the white of one egg, half as much water, and stir in powdered sugar till the paste is stiff. Put the paste between the pieces of walnut.

Peanut Candy.—Chop a quart of shelled peanuts. Butter a broad, shallow pan in the bottom and on the sides and spread the nuts evenly around. Boil one pound of sugar with half a teacup of water, add a pinch of cream tartar, and let boil until it cracks. Pour over the nuts and set aside; when half cool, cut in flat, broad sticks with a sharp knife.

Homemade Candy.—Boil together for half an hour one large teaspoonful of water, two of butter, four of molasses, and nine of sugar. Stir briskly and cool in thin sheets.

Kisses.—Beat the whites of three eggs to a stiff froth, add five spoonfuls of fine white sugar and flavor with lemon. Drop with a spoon on buttered paper, sift sugar over, and bake half an hour in a slow oven.

Vinegar Candy.—Two cups of sugar, one-half cup of water, four tablespoonfuls of vinegar. Stir before putting on the stove, but not after.

St. Louis Butter Taffy.—One cup of sugar, one-half cup of water, one teaspoonful of molasses, two teaspoonfuls of vinegar, butter size of an egg.

Chocolate Caramels.—One cup of grated chocolate, one cup of milk, one cup of molasses, one cup of sugar, butter the size of an egg. Boil all together till it thickens, then cool in shallow pans.

Molasses Taffy.—One-half pint New Orleans molasses, one teaspoonful of soda. Boil, test in water, and when done stir in the soda, pour on plates to cool, and pull until of a pale buff color. If nut candy is desired, stir the kernels in the hot taffy, pour it on plates and cut in squares.

Butter Scotch.—One pound of light brown sugar, one-fourth pound of fresh butter. Boil, but do not stir, when done pour it on plates and cut in squares.

Pickled Watermelon Rind.—For pickles cut into strips about two inches long, soak over night in water with a little salt added, in the morning pour off the water and add one quart of vinegar and one pint of sugar for every gallon of pickles. Cook slowly and stir often till they look clear. Add allspice, cinnamon and cloves to suit the taste. Pickles from ripe cucumbers can be made in the same way.

Sweet Apple Pickles.—Take seven pounds of sweet apples; pare and steam until tender. Place in a pan with three pints of vinegar, three pounds of sugar and half a pint ground spices in equal quantities (cloves, cinnamon and allspice tied loosely in a cloth); cook them as you would preserves. When done, place in a jar, boil down the liquid, and pour over. If there is not enough to cover nicely, make more syrup in the same proportion. The pickles must be well covered.

Sweet Cucumber Pickles.—Take a green cucumber, pare and clean seeds out, soak them in salt brine over night, then in the morning rinse with cold water, to one pint of vinegar add one pinch of brown sugar. Put in as many cucumbers as the vinegar and sugar will take, then take a bag of allspice and put in with the pickles while cooking. Cook all clear, put in jars and cover with greased paper.

Excellent Catsup.—Put tomatoes in a tin kettle, cover close until hot enough to burst, then drain and pass through a sieve. To one quart of pulp add salt, two-thirds wine glass (or less), mustard seed, one-half a teaspoon; ginger, one-half a teaspoon; cayenne pepper to the taste; brandy, a wine glass; vinegar, two-thirds tumbler; whole cloves, one-half wine glass; whole allspice, one-half wine glass; two onions to be taken out whole. Shut tight and boil until of desired thickness.

Walnut Catsup.—Walnut shell juice, three gallons; salt, seven pounds; ginger, eight ounces; garlic, eight ounces; horse radish, eight ounces; essence of anchovies, one quart. Mix.

Pickled Cabbage.—Four large crisp cabbages chopped fine, one quart of onions, enough vinegar to cover, two pounds of brown sugar, two teaspoonfuls of mustard, black pepper, cinnamon, tumeric, celery seed, allspice, mace, pulverized alum. Pack cabbage and onions in alternate layers with a little salt between. Let stand over night; scald vinegar, spices together and pour over cabbage. Do this three mornings, the fourth morning put over the fire and boil five minutes.

Mixed Pickle.—Cut into thin slices half a peck of green tomatoes, one small, hard head of cabbage, six green peppers, one dozen onions, one large root of horse-radish. Put all into a jar, sprinkle thoroughly with salt and let stand for twelve hours, then press the liquor from the mass, and add to the pickle, black and white mustard seed, little ginger root, one ounce of whole allspice, one tablespoonful of ground mustard, pack into a stone jar, and add one quart of good cider vinegar. Ready for use in a week.

Blackberry Pickles.—Seven pounds of berries, three pounds of sugar, one pint of vinegar; cloves and cinnamon to taste, let all come to a boil, then skim out the berries into a jar, boil down the juice, pour on the berries and seal while hot with the white of an egg and flour sack, or put in cans and seal.

Mint Vinegar.—Put into a wide-mouthed bottle fresh, clean mint leaves, enough to fill it loosely; then fill up the bottle with good vinegar, and after it has been stopped close for two or three weeks, it is to be poured off clean into another bottle, and kept well corked for use. Serve with lamb when mint cannot be obtained.

Raspberry Vinegar.—Fill a jar with red raspberries, cover with best cider or apple vinegar. Let it stand ten days, strain through a cloth or sieve, don't press the berries, just let the juice run through; add one pound loaf sugar to every pint of juice;

boil twenty minutes, skim, and bottle when cold. Use a tea-spoon to a glass of water.

Pickled Onions.—After pouring boiling water on them, peel; put them in weak brine, changing it every day for five days; then drain dry. Take vinegar to cover, add pepper, cinnamon, a few cloves, some pieces horseradish; boil all in the vinegar; pour on when cold.

Chili Sauce.—Eighteen ripe tomatoes, one onion, three green peppers, all chopped fine, one cup sugar, two and one-half cups vinegar, two teaspoons salt, one teaspoon each of all kinds of spices. Boil two hours.

Grape Catsup.—Five pounds ripe grapes, two and one-half pounds white sugar, one pint vinegar, one tablespoonful each ground clove, allspice, cinnamon, white pepper, and one-half salt, a saltspoon of cayenne pepper. Pick the grapes over carefully, wash them, put into a porcelain kettle (six or eight quart) with a pint of water, place over a moderate fire; when heated through, with a potato masher mash thoroughly, boil until the pulp is dissolved, stirring often to prevent burning; when the pulp is soft press through a fine pressed tin colander (there should be nothing left but seeds), return to the pot and boil, adding other ingredients; boil until quite thick, stirring continually; when cool bottle and seal.

Pickled Cauliflower.—One cauliflower, boil in salted water until tender; place in an earthen dish; boil one pint vinegar, one cup sugar, six cloves, six whole black peppers, six allspice together, and pour over the cauliflower; to be eaten cold.

Blackberry Pickles.—To four quarts of blackberries, take two quarts of sugar and one pint of vinegar, with three teaspoonfuls each of ground cinnamon and cloves; tie the spices in a cloth, boil all together one hour, then skim out the berries; boil the juice down about one-third, turn over the berries, and keep in a closely covered jar.

Mustard Pickles.—Peel them well, cut them in slices, then take the seeds out, mix them well with salt, and leave them in a dish or bowl all night. The next morning lay them single on a table, let the salt water run off, and then dry each with a clean cloth, then put them in a stone jar, and always put between cloves, onions, allspice, bay leaf, and mustard seed, then boil strong vinegar and let it cool off, then pour it over the pickles.

Mango Peppers.—Cut the ends off the peppers and clean out; soak two days in clear water; one week in salt water; fill with cabbage and inclose.

Grape Catsup.—Wild grapes make delicious catsup, and jelly. Boil grapes until soft, then press through a coarse sieve. To five pounds of grape pulp, add three pounds of sugar, one teaspoonful of cinnamon, one teaspoonful each of cloves, pepper and allspice, one grated nutmeg, one quart of vinegar. Boil slowly until thick as tomato catsup, then bottle.

Piccalilli.—One-half peck of smooth green tomatoes (about two inch diameter nicest size); two medium firm heads of cabbage; slice all as thin as possible, rejecting the stem and blossom parts of the tomatoes, and the coarse leaves of the cabbage. Equal quantities can be taken, or more cabbage than tomatoes, as one prefers. Put into a stone jar alternate layers of tomatoes and cabbage, sprinkle every layer or two with salt (allowing about pint salt to two gallons of pickle). Let stand twelve or fourteen hours, then press and drain out the pickle as dry as possible. Put into a stone jar, putting in cayenne pepper, whole cloves, mustard seed, grated horse radish to suit one's taste, and a little sliced or chopped onion if one likes. Heat boiling hot enough of the best vinegar to cover the pickle, weighting it down with saucer. Reheat the vinegar two or three times, and it will be sure to keep well.

Chili Sauce.—One peck of ripe tomatoes, skinned, six green hot-peppers, six small onions, two teaspoonfuls each of ground allspice, cloves and cinnamon, one cup of sugar, five cups of vinegar, salt to taste. Chop the onions and peppers fine, boil all together slowly four or five hours, then seal up in wide-mouthed bottles.

Mushroom Catsup.—Put a layer of full grown, freshly gathered mushrooms, at the bottom of a deep pan. Sprinkle thickly with salt. Then mushrooms, and salt till all are in the pan. Let them stand three hours. Then mash them well, with the hands, and cover over. Let them stand for two days, stirring up each day well. Put them into a large stone jar. To each quart of mushrooms allow one ounce and a half of black pepper-corns, and half an ounce of whole allspice. Close the jar tightly, and set in a pot of hot water, and let it boil for three hours. Then take out the jar. Pour the juice clear from the settlings, through a hair sieve, without pressing, into a clean pan. Let this juice gently simmer a-half or three-quarters of an hour. Skim it well while cooking. Then pour it through a cloth, and add one table-spoon of good brandy to each pint of catsup. Let it stand as be-fore. Bottle it in half pint bottles. Closely cork. Dip each bot-tle in cement.

Chow Chow.—One peck of green tomatoes, four heads of cabbage, one-half pint small peppers, one dozen medium sized onions, one pint horse radish; grind all together in a sausage grinder, if you have one; if not chop very fine; put in a layer of the ingredients in a dish, then a layer of salt, let stand all night, then drain thoroughly; while draining, put in your porcelain-lined preserving kettle one gallon of good vinegar, a quantity of cloves and allspice tied in a bag, one teacup of sugar, the same of white mustard seed, a little celery seed, one-half ounce of tu-meric acid, and a little salt, if necessary. Let this come to a boil, then add your ingredients, letting all boil together about five minutes, stirring well. When done, pack in a stone jar; this rule will make about two and one-half gallons.

French Pickle.—Twenty four large cucumbers, six red pep-pers, one-fourth peck of beans, one-fourth peck of onions, two large heads of cabbage, one ounce of celery seed, one-fourth pound white mustard seed; one-fourth pound of dry mustard, one cup of sugar, one ounce of tumeric. Boil the cucumbers, etc., in vinegar and water, with salt thrown in, for fifteen minutes, then drain and cool; when cold, add cold vinegar, with the mustard, sugar, tumeric, etc.

PART XI.

Ice Cream, Sherbets and Water Ices.

Neapolitan Ice Cream.—One quart cream, four eggs, one cup sugar, flavoring. Under this name may be included all the varieties made with eggs and cream. The foundation is the same for all, the varieties taking their name from the flavoring used. Directions for preparing the flavoring will be found under each special head.

No. 1. Scald* the cream; beat the yolks till thick and creamy, add the sugar and beat again. Beat the whites stiff, and beat them well into the yolks. Pour the hot cream into the eggs, and when well mixed turn back into the double boiler and cook like a boiled custard. Stir constantly until the foam disappears and the custard has thickened enough to coat the spoon. Strain at once, and when cold add the flavoring and freeze.

No. 2. Make the custard as in No. 1, using the yolks only. Beat the whites until just foamy but not stiff, strain the hot custard into them, beating thoroughly. Or, add the beaten whites when the custard is partly frozen.

Plain Ice Cream.—One pint milk, one cup sugar, two scant tablespoonfuls flour, one pint cream, two eggs, one saltspoonful salt, two tablespoonfuls flavoring. Boil the milk and cream, reserving a quarter of a cup of milk. Mix the sugar, flour and salt thoroughly. Beat the eggs till light, add the cold milk and the sugar mixture, and when well mixed add the boiling milk. Turn back into the double boiler and cook twenty minutes. Stir constantly till smooth, and after that occasionally. Strain through a gravy strainer, add more sugar if needed, and when cold add the flavoring. Freeze as usual. This is a good foundation for an inexpensive cream, and if a larger quantity be desired, more cream and sugar may be added with the flavoring. If the milk be boiling when the flour is added, and cooked

---

*Scald means to heat over hot water till hot, but not boiling. The cup used in this receipt holds half a pint.

thoroughly, there will be no taste of the flour. If you have no cream, use all milk, four eggs, and add one rounding tablespoonful of butter when you take the thickened milk from the fire. The amount of sugar needed will vary with the flavoring.

Hollipin Ice Cream.—Make the Neapolitan ice cream and flavor it with vanilla or almond. When ready to serve cut several vanilla cigarette wafers into two-inch pieces and stick them into the cream.

Maraschino Ice Cream.—Make the Neapolitan ice cream and flavor it with vanilla and a few drops of rose and almond extract. When ready to serve pour a gill of maraschino over the cream, and serve a spoonful of the liquor with each portion of cream.

Macaroon Ice Cream.—Dry one dozen stale macaroons, roll or pound them fine, and sift through a fine gravy strainer. Add them to ice cream made after either receipt and flavored with extract of almond or sherry wine. Stir them in when the cream is partly frozen. Scald the cream if you wish a firm, solid cream.

Ice Cream with Gelatine.—One quart milk, eight eggs, one saltspoon salt, one pint cream, one and a half cups sugar, one-quarter box Nelson's Gelatine, lemon, coffee, wine, or any strong flavoring. Soak the gelatine in half a cup of the measure of cold milk. Boil the remainder of the milk and cream. Beat the eggs till creamy, add the sugar and salt and beat again. Add the hot milk, then put into the double boiler, stir constantly, and cook till it thickens and coats the spoon. Add the soaked gelatine, and more sugar if needed, and when dissolved strain it and set away to cool. When cold, flavor highly with lemon, wine, or any flavoring strong enough to disguise the taste of the gelatine.

Frozen Custard.—One quart milk, one cup sugar, one saltspoonful salt, six or eight eggs (yolks), flavoring. Scald the milk. Beat the yolks till thick and creamy, add the sugar and salt and beat again. Pour the hot milk over them, and when well mixed turn into the double boiler and cook until thick and creamy. Stir constantly and lift the boiler up from the fire occasionally, to check the cooking. Strain at once, and when cool, flavor to taste. This will be greatly improved by adding a little cream (even if it be but half a cupful) just before freezing. When eggs and milk are used without cream in making ice cream, they should always be cooked before freezing. Then the ice cream will be rich, smooth, solid, and fine-grained; but when made without cooking, it will be snowy, mushy, or full of icy particles, and be thin and watery when melted.

Baked Apple Ice Cream.—No. 1. Bake and sift six nice, sweet apples. Add one quart of rich cream and sugar to taste. When the sugar is dissolved, freeze as directed.

No. 2. Bake and sift six tart apples. Add one saltspoonful of cinnamon, one teaspoonful of rose water, one tablespoonful of lemon juice, and sugar to sweeten. Add one quart of cream, scalded, with one cup of sugar. When cool, freeze as usual.

Banana Ice Cream.—Peel six ripe bananas, split and remove the seeds and dark portion in the center. Rub the pulp through a puree strainer. Add to it the juice of one lemon, a saltspoonful of salt, and sugar to make it quite sweet. Add this pulp to either receipt for ice cream, and freeze as usual.

Vanilla Ice Cream.—No. 1. The simplest way to make vanilla ice cream is to make either of the five kinds given as a foundation, and just before freezing flavor with from one to two tablespoonfuls of the vanilla extract. The amount will depend upon the strength and purity of the extract.

No. 2. Make whichever foundation cream is preferred and use a quarter less than the sugar given in the receipt. Just before freezing add from one to two tablespoonfuls of vanilla sugar, or enough to give the flavor desired.

Frozen Pudding.—Any rich ice cream highly flavored with wine, brandy, Jamaica rum, or maraschino, and made quite thick with a variety of fruits, nuts, etc., and served with a cold, rich sauce, may be called a "frozen pudding." Sometimes the cream is molded in cake-lined molds, or served in a hollow loaf of cake (a cake with the inside cut out, leaving an inch thickness of crust on the bottom and sides) and ornamented with whipped cream.

Follow the receipt for ice cream with gelatine. While the cream is cooling prepare the fruit and nuts, and make the sauce.

Use one pound of assorted French fruit; or one pint of brandy peaches; or one pound of mixed raisins. currants and citron; use figs and dates, if you like, or use half fruit and half nuts, almonds, walnuts, or pistachios; or use half fruit or half crumbs of macaroons, dry cake, etc. French fruit should be cut fine and softened by soaking in hot syrup. Canned fruit should be drained and sprinkled with sugar. Dried fruit should be washed, picked over, stoned or seeded, and fine cut. Raisins should be steeped in boiling water, enough to cover, till swollen and tender, then drained, seeded and cut in quarters. Citron should be shaved in small, thin slices, and if very hard, steeped before cutting.

Mix half the fruit and nuts with the frozen cream. Butter a melon mold slightly and line it with lady-fingers or thin sponge cake. Fit it in tightly, then sprinkle a layer of mixed fruit over the cake. Pack the frozen cream in nearly to the top, then the remainder of the fruit, and cover with cake. Cover closely and bind a strip of buttered cloth round the edge of the cover, or cover the edge thick with butter. Pack in ice and salt for one or two hours. When ready to serve dip quickly into warm water and turn out carefully and serve with sauce.

Sauce for Frozen Pudding.—No. 1. Sweeten and flavor a pint of cream. Chill it, and just before serving whip it and skim off the froth.

No. 2. Make a rich boiled custard with one pint of hot cream, the yolks of four eggs, and half a cup of sugar. Flavor with lemon, caramel, or vanilla. Serve it very cold.

Coffee Ice Cream.—Make a quarter of a cup of filtered coffee, or, if you have no filter coffee pot, put two heaping table-spoonfuls of fine ground coffee in a fine strainer placed in a bowl. Then pour through it one-third of a cup of boiling water. Pour the liquid through a second time, and if not clear strain it through a fine cloth. Add this clear liquid to the hot cream or custard, and make the ice cream after either receipt.

No. 2. Steep one-fourth cup of coarsely ground coffee in one pint of cream or milk twenty minutes. Remove it, let it settle, and pour off carefully, then strain it and add it to the remainder of the cream or custard. This is sufficient for one quart of ice cream, made according to either receipt.

Nut Ice Cream.—*Filbert, Hazelnut, or Chestnut.*—Shell and blanch the nuts, then either boil till soft, mash to a pulp and press through a strainer; or roast slightly, chop, pound to a paste and sift; pound again all that does not go through; then cook the nut paste with the cream or custard. Allow one cup of nuts to either receipt for ice cream.

English Walnut.—Shell, blanch, chop fine, sift, and stir into the cream when partly frozen.

American Walnut or Shellbark, and Pecan Nuts.—Shell, chop fine without blanching, sift, and stir them into the cream just before freezing, or as soon as thoroughly chilled. In using pecans avoid taking any of the puckery brown substance which often adheres to the meat. Rinse them quickly in hot water and dry them before chopping.

Butternuts and the three-sided cream nuts are too oily to use in ice cream.

Ice creams made with nuts should be salted more than other creams.

Frozen Apricots.—Cut one can of apricots into small pieces, add one pint of sugar and one quart of water. When the sugar is dissolved, freeze. When it begins to harden, add one pint of whipped cream, measured after whipping. This is delicious without the cream.

Peaches, pineapples, cherries and strawberries are delicious when frozen. Vary the amount of sugar as the fruit requires. These differ from the sherbets in that the fruit is cut in small pieces and not sifted. They may be made with equal parts of fruit and water, with sugar to taste, and a little cream or not, as you please.

Lemon Sherbets.—Four lemons, one pint sugar, one quart boiling water. Shave off the peel from two lemons in thin, wafer-like parings, being careful to take none of the light-colored rind below the oil cells. Put the parings into a bowl, add the boiling water and let it stand ten minutes, closely covered. Cut the lemons in halves, remove the seeds, squeeze out the juice and add it with the sugar to the water. Add more sugar if needed. When cold strain it through a fine strainer into the can and freeze.

Pineapple Sherbet.—One pint of fresh or one can of grated pineapple, one quart sugar, one pint water, one tablespoonful gelatine, one lemon. Pare the pineapple, remove all the eyes, and pick off the tender part with a fork, rejecting all the hard core. If still too coarse, chop it a little. Add the sugar, water, lemon juice, and gelatine, which should be first soaked in cold water and then dissolved in boiling water. Freeze as usual.

Strawberry or Blackberry Sherbet.—One quart berries, or enough to make one pint juice, one pint sugar, one lemon. Mash the berries, add the sugar, and after standing till the sugar is dissolved, add the water and lemon juice. Press through fine cheese-cloth and freeze. Vary the sugar as the fruit requires. All of these fresh fruits are improved by the addition of the lemon.

Lemon Ginger Sherbet.—Cut four ounces of candied ginger in fine pieces and steep it with the lemon, as directed in lemon sherbet.

Lemon Sherbet (with gelatine.)—One tablespoonful gelatine, six lemons, one pint sugar, three and a half cups cold water, half cup boiling water. Soak the gelatine in half a cup of cold water twenty minutes. Put the sugar and the remaining cold water into a large lip bowl or pitcher. Pare the lemons, cut in halves, remove all the seeds, and press out the juice with a lemon-squeezer; add it to the syrup. Dissolve the soaked gelatine in the boiling water, add it to the other mixture. If liked sweeter, add more sugar. When the sugar is dissolved strain through fine wire strainer or cheese-cloth, turn into the freezer can and freeze as directed. Sherbet made in this way has none of the volatile lemon oil, which to a delicate stomach often proves indigestible.

Lemon Sherbet (with white of egg.)—Two quarts boiling water, eight lemons, one egg (white), one quart sugar. Spread part of the sugar on a shallow plate or board, and after wiping the lemons with a clean, damp cloth, roll them in the sugar to extract the oil. Then cut in halves, remove the seeds, and squeeze out the juice. Boil all the sugar and water until clear. Remove the scum as it rises. Add the lemon juice to the syrup, strain it, and pour it gradually into the beaten egg. Then freeze as usual.

Shaddock, or Grape-Fruit Sherbet.—One tablespoonful gelatine, three cups sugar, one pint water, six shaddocks. Soak the gelatine in a little of the cold water fifteen minutes; add the sugar to the remainder, and boil five minutes. Dissolve the soaked gelatine in the boiling syrup. Divide the shaddocks across the sections, remove the seeds, and scoop out the pulp with a teaspoon. Leave all the membranous walls of the sections in the skin. Add the pulp to the cold syrup. Freeze until hard, or only until mushy, as preferred.

Frozen Beverages.—*Coffee.* Prepare two quarts of strong, clear coffee, and sweeten to taste. When cold put it in the freezer and turn the crank until it is like soft mush.

Tea. Prepare one quart of tea, sweeten to taste, and when cool add a little lemon juice. Freeze until mushy.

Eggnog. Beat two eggs till light and creamy, add two tablespoonfuls of sugar and beat again. Add two tablespoonfuls of wine or brandy and one cup of cream or milk. Put in the freezer can and turn the crank until half frozen.

PART XII.

Miscellaneous.

Potato Yeast.—Grate six potatoes, add one cup sugar, one cup salt, pour boiling water until it thickens, about four quarts. When cool, add one pint good yeast. Set in a warm place till well raised. Put away in a stone or glass jar, with thin cloth cover. Set in a cool place and will keep two months. In making bread with this yeast use a little more than of hop yeast.

Egg Plant.—No. 1. Peel it, cut it in slices about half an inch thick, spread salt over each slice, putting one slice on top of the other; let it lie two hours, then wash the salt off of it in cold water, dry it with a towel. Beat two or three eggs, then dip each slice in rolled cracker; fry in boiling hot lard the same as you would doughnuts.

No. 2. Cut the egg plant in slices an inch thick, and let it lie for several hours in salted water to remove the bitter taste. To fry it put the slices in the frying pan with small quantity butter and turn them when one side is done.

Scrappel.—Take four pigs' feet, singe, scrape and wash thoroughly; boil soft, take from the fire, pick out the bones, mash fine, season with salt and pepper, pour all back in the pot, bring to a boil, and thicken with oatmeal or cornmeal; then pour into a net square pan, set aside to cool, cut in slices, to use cold, or, better yet, dip in flour and fry in butter; it is simply delicious; it is also nice made of either veal or chicken.

Baked Macaroni.—Put the macaroni into boiling water, to every quart of which a teaspoon of salt has been added. It will be boiled tender in about twenty minutes. When done, drain, rinse, and lay in cold water. Then place it in a baking dish. Pour over it the following sauce: One ounce each of butter and flour. Stir on the fire till they bubble. Gradually add half a pint of boiling water. Stir the same with an egg-whip until smooth and then season with one teaspoon of salt, and a quarter of a saltspoon of pepper. Dust bread crumbs over the top, put a few pieces of butter on that, and brown quickly in a very hot oven.

Ham Toast.—Mince boiled ham from yesterday dinner very fine, stir in a pint of cream, prefer butter, and mustard and two eggs beaten, boil and pour over nicely browned toast; serve hot.

Ham Toast.—Mix with one tablespoonful of finely chopped or grated ham the beaten-up yolk of an egg, and a little cream and pepper, heat over the fire, and then spread the mixture either on hot, buttered toast, or on slices of bread fried quite crisp in butter; serve very hot.

Egg Sandwiches.—The yolks of two hard-boiled eggs pounded in a mortar with a little chopped, parsley, butter, salt pepper. When of a fine paste, spread on the sandwich bread, and put slices of chicken and small salad chopped.

Ham Sandwich.—Take the pieces of boiled ham which are left after the best of the slices have been cut, and chop fine. Spread this on slices of buttered bread with pepper or mustard according to taste.

Turkey Dressing.—Take two-thirds bread crumbs and one-third fresh mashed potatoes, two eggs, a small piece of butter; season with onions, sage, salt and pepper, stir lightly with a fork.

Dressing for Turkey.—Four crackers, one tablespoonful of sweet marjoram, half a teaspoonful of pepper, a very little clove; add salt and butter the size of an egg.

Raspberry Salad.—Of sweet fruit salads few are more delicious than raspberry, the fruit that more than any other seems to need a syrup or dressing to bring out its delicious flavor. To a quart of raspberries you need half a pint of red currant juice and a gill of clear syrup, made by dissolving a gill of sugar into a saucepan with a tablespoonful of hot water; when melted add the currant juice, when cold pour this over the raspberries, and set on ice till morning.

Tomato Salad.—Take six round, smooth ripe tomatoes, pour over them some boiling water and let them stand in it about two minutes. Then take a sharp knife and peel off all the skin—which has been loosened by the hot water. Set them on ice until they are cold and firm. Then, with a sharp knife, cut them in even round slices, but do not separate; let each tomato, though cut, remain in its original shape. Set each on a round scalloped dish in a little nest of the inner leaves of a crisp lettuce, about three leaves to each tomato. Then pour over them a nice mayonnaise sauce.

Mince Meat.—One-half pound of raw beefsteak (no skin or fat) well chopped, one-half pound of beef suet chopped, one pound of stoned raisins, one pound of cleaned currants, one and one-fourth pound apples peeled, cored and chopped, one-half pound of citron and orange peel chopped fine, one and one-half pounds of brown sugar, one dessert spoon of salt to draw out the flavor, one small nutmeg, one tablespoon of allspice, a little brandy is liked by some, an extra half pound of sugar will keep the mince meat as well as brandy. This is ready for immediate use, but keeping improves it.

Mince Meat.—Four pounds chopped meat, one pound suet, nine pounds apples, three pounds raisins, two pounds currants, five pounds sugar, three teaspoons cloves, ten teaspoons cinnamon, two nutmegs, two teaspoons black pepper, five tablespoons salt, one quart boiled cider, one quart molasses.

Mince Meat.—Boil solid piece of beef till very tender, add salt while boiling, chop very fine. To one bowl of meat add two heaping bowls of chopped russet apples, sweeten with sugar to taste. Mix with good strong cider, one and a-half pounds of seeded raisins, one-half pound of currants washed thoroughly. Pour over them cider enough to boil slowly about fifteen minutes; when cold add them to the mince meat. Flavor with cloves, allspice, nutmeg and cinnamon. In using the cider put only enough to mix the ingredients, then moisten thoroughly with good French brandy. The pies should be baked slowly one hour.

Rice a la Fromage.—Boil one cupful of rice, strain and dry. In a baking dish put a layer of rice, pepper and salt. Grate one-fifth of a pound of mild cheese, sprinkle some over the rice in layers until all is used. Beat an egg with one-half cup of milk and pour over the contents of the dish. Spread bread crumbs on top, drop a teaspoonful of melted butter over. Bake until nicely browned.

Mince Meat.—Two pounds fresh lean beef, boiled, and when cold chopped fine, three-fourths pound beef suet chopped very fine, four pounds of apples, pared and chopped, one and one-half pounds of raisins, one pound of currants, well washed; three-fourths pound of citron shaved fine, mace, clover, cinnamon, nutmeg, allspice, sugar and salt to taste, one pint of boiled cider, mix thoroughly, using enough of the liquor in which the meat was boiled, to moisten it, heat all together, and when done, pour in a stone jar, keep closely covered in a cool, dry place; if a larger batch is required, double the receipe; you can add a little brandy if preferred to the last.

Chow Chow.—One quart large cucumbers, one quart small cucumbers, two quarts onions, four heads cauliflower, six green peppers, one quart green tomatoes, one gallon vinegar, one pound mustard, two cups sugar, two cups flour, one ounce turmeric. Put all in salt and water one night; cook all the vegetables in brine until tender, except large cucumbers. Pour over vinegar and spices.

Pickling Cauliflowers.—Take whitest and closest cauliflowers in bunches; spread on earthen dish, cover them with salt, and let stand three days to draw out all the water. Then put in jars, pour boiling salt and water over them, let stand over night; then drain with a hair sieve, and put in glass jars; fill up jars with vinegar; cover tight.

East India Pickles.—One hundred cucumbers (large and small) one peck green tomatoes, half peck onions, four cauliflowers, four red peppers (without seeds), four heads celery, one pint bottle horse-radish. Slice all, stand in salt twenty-four hours; then drain, pour over weak vinegar, stand on stove until it comes to a boil, then drain again. One ounce ground cinnamon, one ounce ground turmeric, pound mustard, quarter pound brown sugar; wet these with cold vinegar; add sufficient vinegar to moisten all the pickles. Cook all together ten minutes. Seal in bottles while hot.

Pickled Red Cabbage.—Slice it into a colander, sprinkle each layer with salt; let it drain two days, then put into a jar, pour boiling vinegar enough to cover, put in a few slices of red beet-root. Choose purple red cabbage. Those who like flavor of spice will boil it, with the vinegar. Cauliflower cut in bunches, and thrown in after being salted, will look red and beautiful.

French Pickles.—One peck green tomatoes, sliced; six large onions, teacup salt thrown on over night. Drain thoroughly, boil in two quarts water and one quart vinegar fifteen or twenty minutes; drain in colander; then take four quarts vinegar, two pounds brown sugar, half pound white mustard seed, two table-spoonfuls cloves, two tablespoonfuls cinnamon, two tablespoon-fuls ginger, two tablespoonfuls ground mustard, teaspoonful cayne pepper; put all together, cook fifteen minutes.

Mangoes.—Take small musk melons and cut an oval piece out of one side; take out the seeds with teaspoon, and fill this space with stuffing of chopped onion, scraped horse-radish, mustard seed, cloves, and whole pepper; sew in the piece. Put in jar, pour boiling vinegar, with a little salt in it, over them. Do this three times, then put in fresh vinegar, cover close.

Pickles.—Use glass bottles for pickles, also wooden knives and forks in preparation of them. Fill bottles three parts full with articles to be pickled, then fill bottle with vinegar. Use sauce-pans lined with earthenware, or stone pipkins, to boil vinegar in.

Pickled Peaches.—Take ripe, but not too soft peaches, put a clove into one end of each peach. Take two pounds brown sugar to gallon of vinegar, skim and boil up twice; pour it hot over peaches and cover close. In a week or two pour off and scald vinegar again. After this they will keep any length of time.

To Pickle Cucumbers.—Take two or three hundred, lay them on a dish, salt, and let them remain eight or nine hours; then drain, laying them in a jar, pour boiling vinegar upon them. Place near the fire, covered with vine-leaves. If they do not become sufficiently green, strain off the vinegar, boil it, and again pour it over them, covering with fresh leaves. Continue till they become green as you wish.

To Pickle Tomatoes.—Always use those that are thoroughly ripe. The small round ones are decidedly the best. Do not prick them, as most books direct. Let them lie in strong brine three or four days, then put down in layers in jars, mixing with small onions and pieces of horse-radish. Then pour on vinegar (cold), which should be first spiced; let there be a spice-bag to

throw into every pot. Cover carefully, and set by in cellar full
month before using.

Sweet Pickles for Plums, Peaches or Tomatoes.—Four
quarts cider vinegar, five pounds sugar, quarter pound cinnamon, two ounces cloves to seven pounds fruit. Scald the vinegar
and sugar together and skim, add spices, boil up once, and pour
over the fruit. Pour off and scald vinegar twice more at inter-
vals of three days, and then cover all close. A less expensive
way: Take four pounds sugar to eight pounds of fruit, two ounces
cinnamon, one ounce cloves, one teaspoon salt, one teaspoonful
allspice.

Brandy Peaches.—Drop peaches in hot water, let them remain till skin can be ripped off; make thin syrup, let it cover
fruit; take it out, make very rich syrup, and add, after it is taken
from the fire, while it is still hot, an equal quantity of brandy.
Pour while still warm over the peaches in the jar. Peaches must
be covered with it.

Canned Pineapple.—Pare fruit—be very particular to cut
out eyes. Weigh and chop fine. Add same weight of sugar.
Mix thoroughly in large crock, let it stand twenty-four hours.
Then put in cans, fill full, seal tight. After leaving them about
three weeks look and see if any signs of working. If so, pour
into pan, warm through, then replace in cans.

Spiced Tomatoes.—Twenty pounds of ripe tomatoes scalded
and peeled, two quarts vinegar, eight pounds sugar, four tablespoonfuls each of cinnamon, cloves, and allspice. Boil till
thick, stirring often.

Spiced Currants.—Five pounds currants, four pounds brown
sugar, two tablespoonfuls cloves, two tablespoonfuls cinnamon,
one pint vinegar; boil two hours or till quite thick.

Spiced Peaches.—Seven pounds fruit, one pint vinegar,
three pounds sugar, two ounces cinnamon, half ounce cloves.
Scald together sugar, vinegar and spices; pour over the fruit.
Let stand twenty-four hours; drain off, scald again and pour over
fruit, letting it stand another twenty-four hours. Boil all together until fruit is tender. Skim it and boil liquor until
thickened. Pour over fruit and set away in jar.

Spiced Grapes.—Seven pounds grapes, three pounds sugar, one pint vinegar, one tablespoonful cloves, one tablespoonful cinnamon.

Spiced Elderberries.—Take nine pounds cleaned elder berries, three pounds brown sugar, one pint vinegar, one ounce cloves, one ounce allspice, one ounce cinnamon; put sugar and vinegar in a two-gallon brass or copper kettle, and place it on the stove; let it come to a boil, then add berries and let it boil two-and-a-half hours; when done grind spice, and tie in little bags and put in; simmer a few minutes, take off and seal in cans.

Pickled Peaches or Pears.—One quart vinegar to four-and-a-half pounds sugar, half pound sugar to little over one pound fruit; place all the sugar and vinegar over the fire till it comes to a boil; then lay a layer of fruit and cook it until soft enough to run a fork through; then remove the fruit and fill the same way until all are done; the syrup needs no more cooking; before cooking the fruit, stick four cloves in each.

To Roast a Fowl.—Time, one hour. One large fowl, two or three large spoonfuls bread crumbs, pepper and salt, half pound butter. Prepare fowl for roasting; put into inside bread crumbs, seasoned with pepper, salt, and piece of butter size of large walnut. Roast at a clear fire, basting well with butter; just before done, dredge with flour, and baste again with butter. When done, add little warm water to butter in dripping-pan, or a little *very thin* melted butter, and strain over fowl. Serve with bread sauce, or little gravy in tureen if preferred.

Goose.—This requires keeping, the same as fowls, some days before cooking. The goose is best in the Autumn and early part of Winter—never good in Spring. What is called a green goose is four months old. It is insipid after that, though tender. Pick well and singe the goose, then clean carefully. Put the liver and gizzard on to cook as a turkey's. When the goose is washed, and ready for stuffing, have boiled three white potatoes, skin and mash them; chop three onions very fine, throw them into cold water; stir into the potatoes a spoonful of butter, a little salt and black pepper, a tablespoonful of finely-rubbed sage leaves; drain off the onions and mix with the potato, sage, etc. When well mixed, stuff the goose with the mixture. Have ready a coarse needle and thread, and sew up the slit made for cleaning and introducing the stuffing. A full-grown goose requires one-and-three-quarter hours. Roast it as a turkey, dredging and basting. The gravy is prepared as for poultry, with the liver and gizzard. Apple-sauce is indispensable for roast goose.

Roast Goose or Duck.—Singe, draw and truss fowl; if an old one parboil it; best stuffing for a goose is sage and onions. If a strong flavor of onions is liked, they should be chopped raw. If this is not the case, should be boiled in one or two waters, and mixed with bread crumbs, powdered sage, salt, pepper, and extract of nutmeg to taste. Fill bird with stuffing, sew up with coarse thread, sprinkle salt over, and set in pan with a little warm water. Baste frequently, and do not take from oven until thoroughly cooked.

Chicken Pâtés.—Chop meat of cold chicken fine and season well. Make large cupful rich drawn butter, and while on fire stir in two eggs, boiled hard, minced very fine, also a little chopped parsley, then chicken meat. Let almost boil. Have ready some pâté-pans of good paste, baked quickly to light brown. Slip from pans while hot, fill with mixture and set in oven to heat. Arrange upon dish and serve hot.

Boned Chicken.—Boil a chicken in little water as possible until meat will fall from bones; remove all skin, chop together light and dark parts; season with pepper and salt. Boil down liquid in which chicken was boiled, then pour it on meat; place in tin, wrap tightly in cloth, press with heavy weight several hours. When served, cut in thin slices.

Chicken Pot-pie.—Two large chickens jointed and boiled in two quarts water; add a few slices salt pork, season. When nearly cooked, add crust made of one quart flour, four teaspoonfuls Royal Baking Powder, one saltspoonful salt; stir in stiff batter with water; drop into kettle while boiling; cover close and cook twenty-five minutes.

Turkey Hash and Poached Eggs.—Cold fowl may be turned into hot breakfast dish as follows: Chop meat very fine, put half pint gravy into stew-pan with little piece of butter rolled in flour, teaspoonful catsup, some pepper, and salt, and peel of half lemon, shred very fine; put in turkey or chicken, and shake over clear fire till thoroughly hot. Above proportions are for cold turkey. It may be served with two or more poached eggs. If there are not eggs enough to allow one for each guest, they should be broken with spoon and mixed with hash just before serving. Serve hot.

Hints on Cooking Vegetables.—First—Have them fresh as possible. Summer vegetables should be cooked on same day they are gathered. Second—Look them over and wash well, cutting out all decayed or unripe parts. Third—Lay them when peeled in cold water for some time before using. Fourth—Always let water boil before putting them in, and continue to boil until done.

Turnips.—Should be peeled, and boiled from forty minutes to an hour.

Beets.—Boil from one to two hours; then put in cold water and slip skin off.

Spinach.—Boil twenty minutes

Parsnips.—Boil from twenty to thirty minutes.

Onions.—Best boiled in two or three waters; adding milk the last time.

String Beans.—Should be boiled one hour.

Shell Beans.—Require half hour to an hour.

Green Corn.—Boil twenty or thirty minutes.

Green Peas.—Should be boiled in little water as possible; boil twenty minutes.

Asparagus.—Same as peas; serve on toast with cream gravy.

Winter Squash.—Cut in pieces and boil twenty to forty minutes in small quantity of water; when done, press water out, mash smooth, season with butter, pepper and salt.

Cabbage.—Should be boiled from half hour to one hour in plenty of water; salt while boiling.

Asparagus on Toast.—Cut stalks of equal length, rejecting woody portions and scraping the whiter parts retained. Tie in bunch with soft tape and cook about thirty minutes, if of fair size; if small, twenty minutes. Have ready six or eight slices nicely toasted bread. Dip in asparagus liquor, butter well and lay on hot dish. Drain the asparagus; untie and arrange on toast. Pepper and salt to taste.

Food for the Sick.—Always prepare food for the sick in the neatest and most careful manner. In sickness the senses are un-usually acute, and far more susceptible to carelessness, negligence and mistakes in the preparation and serving of food then when in health. Special wants of the body show themselves in special cravings for certain articles of food. These should be gratified when possible.

Infants' Food.—Let one quart of milk stand over night ; skim off the cream, and upon it pour one pint of boiling water. In one quart of water let one tablespoonful of oatmeal boil about two hours and then strain. To one gill of the cream and water add two tablespoonfuls of the oatmeal water. Sweeten it when given. This receipt comes from an experienced nurse, and has been well tested.

Flaxseed Tea.—Upon an ounce of unbruised flaxseed and a little pulverized liquorice root pour a pint of boiling (soft or rain) water, and place the vessel containing these ingredients near, but not on, the fire for four hours. Strain through linen cloth. Make it fresh every day. An excellent drink in fever accompanied by a cough.

Mint Tea.—In an earthen vessel put a handful of the young shoots of mint, pour over them boiling water, cover closely and let it set near the fire for an hour. Other herb teas are made in the same way. Mint tea is useful in allaying nausea and vomiting.

Mutton Broth.—Three pounds of lean mutton, two turnips, one carrot, two onions, one bunch parsley, one cup milk, one tablespoonful corn starch, three quarts water. Boil meat, cut into strips, and the vegetables, sliced, in the water two-and-a-half hours. The water should be reduced one-third. Strain, taking out the meat, and rubbing the vegetables to a pulp through the colander. Cool, skim, season, and return to the fire. Heat, stir in the corn starch, wet up with water, and pour into the tureen. Add the milk boiling hot. Stir well and serve.

Welsh Rarebit.—Select richest and best American cheese, the milder the better, as melting brings out strength. To make five rarebits, take one pound cheese, grate and put in tin or porcelain lined saucepan; add ale (old is best) enough to thin the cheese sufficiently, say about a wineglassful to each rarebit. Place over fire, stir until it is melted. Have slice of toast ready for each rarebit (crusts trimmed); put a slice on each plate, and pour cheese enough over each piece to cover it. Serve while hot.

Chicken a l'Italienne.—*Common Batter*, remains of chicken, twelve tomatoes, one cup broth, two tablespoonfuls onion chopped, one tablespoonful parsley, one saltspoonful each salt, white pepper, Royal thyme, and Summer savory, one tablespoonful butter. Cut remains of chicken into small pieces; dip into batter, and fry crisp in plenty of lard made hot for the purpose; serve with *Tomato Sauce*.

Onions, Fried.—After clearing off tops and tails, slice them with a sharp knife; place in pan with beef dripping or good butter. Stir and shake them until they begin to brown. If served with steak, dish and lay the onions on top of the steak; cover, and let stand where they will keep hot, for five minutes, then serve.

Beets.—Use care in cutting off the tops and washing them not to break the skins, or they will bleed away their color in the water. Cook in boiling water one hour. Scrape, slice, salt, pepper and butter, and pour a few spoonfuls of boiling vinegar upon them after they are dished.

Eggs and Asparagus.—Cut about two dozen stalks of asparagus, leaving out the hard parts, into inch lengths, and boil tender. Drain; pour upon them a cupful drawn butter; stir until hot, then turn into a bake dish. Break six eggs upon the top; put a bit of butter upon each; salt and pepper, and put into a quick oven until the eggs are "set."

Eggs with Mushrooms.—Slice the mushrooms from cans into halves. Stew ten minutes in a little butter seasoned with pepper and salt, and a very little water. Drain, put the mushrooms into a pie dish; break enough eggs to cover them over the top; pepper, salt, and scatter bits of butter over them; strew with bread crumbs, and bake until the eggs are "set." Serve in the dish.

Ragout of Vegetables.—Parboil one carrot, one turnip, two potatoes, two ears of corn, one cup of Lima beans, and the same of peas, one onion, and with them quarter pound of fat salt pork. Drain off the water and lay aside the pork. Slice carrots, turnips, potatoes and onion. Put into a saucepan with a cup of some good meat soup before it has been thickened. Season well; cut the corn from the cob and add with the peas, beans, and a sliced tomato as soon as the rest are hot. Stew all together half hour. Stir in a great lump of butter rolled in flour. Stew five minutes, and serve in a deep dish.

Baked Macaroni.—Break half pound of macaroni in pieces an inch long, cook in boiling water, slightly salted, twenty minutes. Drain, and put a layer in bottom of a greased bake dish, upon this some grated cheese and tiny bits of butter; then more macaroni, and so on, filling dish, with grated cheese on top. Wet with a little milk and salt lightly. Cover and bake half hour; brown, and serve in a bake dish.

Boston Brown Bread.—Set a sponge over night with potatoes, or white flour, in the following proportions:

One cup yeast; six potatoes, mashed fine with three cups of flour; one quart warm water; six level teaspoonfuls Cottolene (*or*, if you leave out the potatoes, one quart of warm water to three pints of flour); two tablespoonfuls brown sugar.

Beat up well, and let it rise five or six hours. When light sift into the bread-tray—

One quart rye-flour; two quarts Indian-meal; one tablespoonful salt; one teaspoonful soda or saleratus.

Mix this up very soft with the risen sponge, adding warm water, if needed, and working in gradually half a tea-cupful of molasses.

Knead well, and let it rise from six to seven hours. Then work over again, and divide into loaves, putting these into well-greased, round, deep pans. The second rising should last an hour, at the end of which time bake in a moderate oven about four hours. Rapid baking will ruin it. If put in late in the day, let it stay in the oven all night.

To Bake a Turkey.—Let the turkey be picked, singed, and washed, and wiped dry, inside and out; joint only to the first joint in the legs, and cut some of the neck off if it is all bloody; then cut one dozen small gashes in the fleshy parts of the turkey—on the outside and in different parts—and press one whole oyster in each gash, then close the skin and flesh over each gash as tightly as possible; then stuff your turkey, leaving a little room for the stuffing to swell. When stuffed, sew it up with a stout cord, rub over lightly with flour, sprinkle a little salt and pepper on it, and put some in your dripping-pan; put in your turkey, baste it often with its own drippings; bake to a nice brown; thicken your gravy with a little flour and water. Be sure and keep the bottom of the dripping-pan covered with water or it will burn the gravy and make it bitter.

Stewed Cranberries.—Wash and look over carefully. Place in saucepan, little more than covered with water. Cover saucepan and stew until skins are tender, adding more water if necessary; add one pound sugar to each pound of berries. Let them simmer ten or twelve minutes, then set away in a bowl or wide-mouthed crock.

Fried Spring Chicken.—Clean and joint, then soak in salt water for two hours. Put in frying-pan equal parts of lard and butter—in all enough to cover chicken. Roll each piece in flour, dip in beaten egg, then roll in cracker crumbs, and drop into the boiling fat. Fry until browned on both sides. Serve on flat platter garnished with sprigs of parsley. Pour most of fat from frying-pan, thicken the remainder with browned flour, add to it cup of boiling water or milk. Serve in gravy-boat.

Apple Sauce.—Pare, core, and slice tart apples, stew in water enough to cover them until they break to pieces. Beat to a pulp with a good lump of butter and plenty of sugar; serve cold.

PART XIII.

Little Secrets, Kinks and Wrinkles.

"Cooking means the knowledge of Medea, and of Circe, and of Calypso, and of Helen, and of Rebekah, and of the Queen of Sheba. It means the knowledge of all herbs, and fruits, and balms, and spices, and of all that is healing and sweet in fields and groves and savory in meats; it means carefulness and inventiveness, and watchfulness, and willingness and readiness of appliance; it means the economy of your grandmothers and the science of modern chemists; it means much tasting and no wasting; it means English thoroughness, French art, and Arabian hospitality; and it means in fine, that you are perfectly and always ladies—' loaf givers '—and as you are to see imperatively that everybody has something pretty to put on, so you are to see, yet more imperatively, that everybody has something nice to eat."—*Ruskin.*

Economy counts nowhere for so much as in the kitchen.

For the management of household work, it is the ignorance of minor details and the neglect of little things that causes loss of time, patience and money. Women, therefore, can have no higher aim in life than to acquire a knowledge of the proper performance of the tasks before them.

The information here given of the many little secrets of household management, the Kinks and Wrinkles of Kitchen lore, will be of value to housekeepers seeking aid on the subject.

For making cake, success is only possible when attention is given to details. Accuracy in proportioning the ingredients is of first importance, and everything should be weighed or measured before beginning, as well as the oven heated at the proper temperature.

Butter and sugar must be creamed together; the whites and yolks of eggs beaten separately; the flour sifted twice, and always measured after sifted; the baking powder added the last time; currants require to be washed, dried and floured before using; raisins seeded, citron thinly sliced and freely floured.

Pans and moulds should be greased with lard or cottolene instead of butter. Sweet milk is always used for mixing with baking powder, and makes firm, solid cake; sour milk with soda makes light, spongy cake. An earthen crock should be used for mixing cake batter, and a wooden spoon for beating; sponge cake requires a quick oven, cakes made with butter a moderate oven. A pan of cold water set in the oven will prevent cakes burning or baking too rapidly.

Butter should not be melted before adding to cake. A pinch of salt put in the whites of eggs will make them froth more readily. The oven door should not be opened and closed while a cake is baking. If necessary to look at it, the cake should not be moved until well set. When a cake is done, it should be turned out gently on an inverted sieve, and allowed to cool without handling.

After icing a cake, if it is set in the oven for one or two minutes it will be smooth and white.

Milk makes a whiter bread than water, and bread made with it retains moisture longer.

A fourth of a cake of compressed yeast is equal to two tablespoonsful of liquid yeast.

Compressed yeast, when fresh, is more satisfactory in making bread than home-made yeast.

To test the quality of flour, press a little in the hand; if good it will be light and elastic; the best grades of flour are of a yellowish tinge. In mixing bread use one measure of liquid to three of flour to make a soft dough. Equal quantities of flour and liquid is required for batter. If a sponge is first made and let rise, less flour will be needed in making bread. When set to rise, bread dough should be kept at an even temperature. After being moulded in the pan, the dough should be allowed to double in bulk before putting in the oven.

In making light rolls, kneading will not be necessary if the dough is rolled with the rolling pin, and cut out. Rolls will be lighter if brushed over freely with butter, instead of shorting when mixing. Rolls, buns and rusks require a quick oven and rapid baking. A loaf of bread when done will not burn the hands when turned out of the pan; the crust of a well baked loaf of bread should be a rich brown.

Bread as soon as baked should be taken from the pans, and placed uncovered in such a position as will expose the greatest possible amount of the surface to the air in order to prevent the crust from being hard, as well as permit the rapid escape of gas involved in the process of fermentation.

Stale bread makes excellent pan cakes, griddle cakes, muffins and puddings, and if rolled and sifted can be used instead of crackers for rolling oysters, croquettes, fish or other articles in before frying.

Meat for making soup should always be put on in soft, cold water, which should simmer, not boil; when vegetables are used, they should be added only in time to cook done. For soup, potatoes and cabbage require to be boiled in separate water before being put in the soup; onions will impart a better flavor if first fried in butter. Salt should never be added to soup until it is done, as it hardens the water. For seasoning soups, herbs, spices, cayenne and black pepper are used. Lemon juice gives a slight piquancy, and aids in blending other flavors.

Quenelles and force meat balls are an addition to soup, giving it a pleasing variety. If egg thickening is added to soup, it should be taken up at once, or it will curdle. Croutons or fried bread sippets are served with all clear soups.

A variety of delicious cream soups are made without meat or stock.

In buying beef, select that which is a clear red color, and the fat straw color. When meat pressed by the fingers rises up quickly it is prime. Good mutton is fat, hard and white; the best hams have a thin skin and solid fat.

Young ducks and geese feel tender under the wings, and the web of the feet is supple.

Turkeys and chickens when fresh are white and plump, with moist skin.

Pork at its best must be fine grained, with both fat and lean white.

For boiling fresh meat of any kind the water should be boiling hot, and sufficient to entirely cover the meat; the pot should be amply large, giving room for the water to entirely surround as well as cover the meat. If kept closely covered time and fuel will be saved in boiling meat.

Meat should not be washed before cooking, as the flavor is injured, and the nutriment decreased. Soft water should be used for boiling meat. Salt should not be added to boiling meat until well done. Freshly butchered meat requires a longer time to cook than that killed for a day or two. Meat should never be pierced with a fork in taking up. A stout string should be tied around the joint when first put in the water to keep it in shape, and to lift it when done.

For stews stone jars are better than saucepans.

Rapid cooking and intense heat are injurious to meats.

In seasoning roast or boiled meats add pepper and herbs in the beginning, salt when the meat is nearly done.

Salt meats should be put on to boil in cold water. Ham to be served cold should be allowed to cool in the water in which it is boiled. The time for boiling is usually about twenty minutes to the pound for fresh meat, and thirty minutes to the pound for salt meat, the time varying, of course, according to the quality of the meat. For roasting meat the oven should be hot; fifteen minutes for every pound is allowed for beef and mutton, twenty minutes to the pound for veal, lamb and pork. All meats should be frequently basted while baking. For broiling meat have the fire bright, turn often, and do not season until done. To properly fry meat it should be immersed in boiling fat. To fry in a little grease is saúteing; the latter is the usual mode, and is better for cooking meats than frying. To thaw frozen meat, place in a warm room over night, or lay for a few hours in fresh spring water. Meat once frozen should never be thawed until ready to cook. To keep meat fresh in warm weather sprinkle with a little powdered borax, fold in a cloth and hang up in a cool cellar.

The most suitable garnishes for meats are sliced lemon, pickled beets, parsley, currant, cranberry and grape jellies.

For dressing game and poultry, they should never be washed. but wiped with a damp towel. Birds should be dry picked.

White meated game should be cooked well done, dark meated rare.

All varieties of game are improved in flavor and rendered more tender by keeping.

The usual garnishes for game are sliced oranges, apple sauce, cucumber pickles, preserved barberries and currant jelly.

All green vegetables are better cooked in soft, freshly boiled water, to which a little salt is added. If hard water must be used, half a teaspoonful of soda added to every gallon of water will make it soft. Potatoes should be pared sparingly; when old they are improved by soaking in cold water before boiling; new potatoes are best baked; onions should be soaked in warm salt water for half an hour before cooking. Turnips, carrots and onions should never be split lengthwise, but sliced in rounds, cut across the fibre. Green peas should be shelled, and cooked at once. If green vegetables must be used after wilting, they may be freshened by soaking for an hour or two in clear, cold water. A little sugar added to pease, young corn, turnips and squash is an improvement.

For preparing asparagus for cooking, do not break, but cut off the stalks.

Sweet potatoes require a longer time to cook than white potatoes. When vegetables are to be cooked with salt meat, the meat should be cooked nearly done first, and the vegetables put in the water.

Vegetables should always be thoroughly cooked, and require a longer time late in the season than in Summer.

A half a pod of red pepper dropped into the kettle will destroy the unpleasant odor of cabbage and greens.

Rice should be put on to cook in boiling salt water, and boiled rapidly until done, without stirring.

Macaroni should be cooked in boiling salt water, drained and thrown in cold water for ten minutes to bleach.

For mixing salad dressing use a silver or wooden spoon or fork; vegetables used for salad are, asparagus, cabbage, lettuce, celery, dandelion, water cress, cauliflower, potatoes, tomatoes, string beans, cucumbers and beets. French dressing is used for all vegetable or light salads. Some cooks prefer mayonnaise dressing for tomatoes, celery and cauliflower. Mayonnaise is appropriate for all meat and fish salads. Melted butter or rich cream may be used as a substitute for oil in making salad dressing if preferred. The crispness of vegetables for salads may be preserved by throwing them into ice water for half an hour. Salads should never be mixed with the dressing until ready to serve, and should be very cold. Hard boiled eggs cut into rings, sliced boiled beets, tiny radishes, celery tips, water cress and pickles are suitable garnishes for salads. The usual proportion of oil and vinegar for salad dressing is three parts of oil to one of vinegar.

To ascertain the freshness of an egg before breaking it, hold up toward the sun ; if fresh the yolk is round, the white clear. The shell of a fresh egg always looks porous and dull.

A teaspoonful of vinegar added to the water in which eggs are poached will make them set properly, and prevent the whites spreading.

A perfectly fresh egg will require a longer time to boil than one kept for a day or two.

For soft boiling eggs require from two to three minutes; for hard boiling ten minutes.

For omelets, give the eggs after breaking into a bowl, twelve vigorous beats.

Always use a smooth pan for cooking omelets.

Ham, tongue, oysters or vegetables may be added to a plain omelet to give variety to the breakfast or luncheon table.

A supply of stock should always be kept on hand for making sauces and gravies.

For thickening sauces, the butter and flour should be well mixed, and cooked together before adding the liquid. All flavoring should harmonize and be perfectly blended.

Sauces should be continually stirred while cooking. Brown and white sauces are the foundations of most sauces, which are given their individuality by various seasoning.

Pastry should be mixed with ice water, and handled as little as possible. A marble slab is the best pastry board, and a glass rolling pin the best for rolling out. Puff paste may be kept on ice for two or three days. All pastry is improved by keeping on ice until perfectly chilled, but should never be allowed to freeze.

To prevent the juice of fruit pies from soaking into the under crust, rub over with well beaten egg before filling the crust. To prevent the juice escaping from very juicy filling, pass an inch wide strip of white cotton around the pie when ready for the oven.

To glaze pastry, when half baked take it out of the oven, brush it over with the beaten yolk of an egg and put back until the glaze is set.

For making cream pies, the crust should be baked before the cream is put in it.

Rhubarb if scalded for a few minutes before being put in the crust will require less sugar.

Chess pie should be cut as soon as baked, when it will not fall.

Patty cases should always be baked before filling.

Boiled puddings are lighter when boiled in a cloth, room being allowed for the pudding to swell. Boiled puddings require double the time needed for baking puddings.

For freezing ices allow two quarts of coarse salt to eight pounds of ice. Cream should never be frozen too rapidly. Fruit and flavoring should never be added to cream until half frozen. For making water ices the sugar and water should be boiled until a syrup is formed. It requires a longer time to freeze water ices and sherbets than cream or puddings.

Fruit jellies may be used in the place of fresh fruit juices in making sherbets and water ices.

Mousses are lighter and more spongy than ice creams, and are moulded on ice instead of frozen.

Sorbets should be frozen to a less solid consistence than other ices, and are firm enough when they can be piled in glasses.

In making gelatine jellies the gelatine should be soaked in cold water for one hour before using.

A bag through which to strain jelly is best made of very thin flannel.

The fruit for jellies should be a little under rather than over ripe, and freshly gathered.

Berries and all juicy fruits will require no water in cooking.

One quart of ripe berries will yield one pint of juice.

Jelly should be kept in a cool, dark place.

In making preserves small fruits should be cooked slowly for half an hour, large fruits pared, quartered and boiled slowly in syrup until tender and transparent.

The vinegar for pickles should not be boiled, but simply scalded. A small piece of alum added to pickles will make them crisp and green.

The flavorings for pickles are onions, horseradish, garlic, cayenne, mace, cloves, cinnamon and ginger.

All pickles should be put in glass or stone jars, and kept in a cool, dark place.

Mangoes are best made from peaches and small melons.

Tomatoes for catsup should be gathered in dry weather.

Walnuts for catsup should be young and tender.

A little powdered assafetida added to ripe tomato catsup imparts a delicious flavor.

To make good coffee use water at the first boil. If boiled coffee is used, one minute is the time it should be allowed to boil.

Tea should be drawn, not boiled. A china tea pot is better than a metal one.

Russian tea is made by putting a slice of lemon in the bottom of each cup and pouring boiling tea over it.

Iced tea should be made very strong, allowed to cool after being poured off the leaves, and poured in glasses half filled with shaved ice.

Chocolate is best served with whipped cream.

To blanch almonds, shell, throw them in boiling water, and let stand on the back of the range for five minutes, then take up, drain, put in cold water and rub off the skins. To salt almonds, blanch and spread them on a tin dish, add a teaspoonful of butter and stand in a moderate oven for ten minutes, or until a light brown. Peanuts may be salted in the same way.

To make caramel for coloring soups and sauces, stir a cup full of granulated sugar in an iron saucepan over the fire until brown, add a cup full of boiling water, let boil one minute, pour into a bottle and cork tightly.

To clarify sugar put the sugar and water on to boil, mix the white of an egg with a little water, add to the boiling syrup, let come to a boil and skim.

To scald milk put it in a double boiler or a small tin bucket, stand it in a deep pan of boiling water over the fire; when it begins to steam take it up.

To clarify fat put the scraps of fat and the drippings to be clarified into a saucepan, set over a moderate fire until melted, strain into a saucepan; to every two pounds add a teacup of boiling water and a small pinch of soda. Stand over the fire and let boil until the water has evaporated and the grease is clear. Skim, strain and set away to cool.

To keep berries cover with cold water, changing it every day.

To keep cheese moist dip a linen cloth in wine vinegar, and wrap the cheese in it.

To freshen salt fish, soak in sour milk over night.

To make old fowls and tough meat tender add a spoonful of vinegar to the water in which they are boiled.

To remove the smell of onions, cabbage and greens from kettles, put wood ashes in them, fill with boiling water and let stand until cool; or add powdered borax to the water in the place of ashes.

To clean a frying pan, wipe out with a piece of soft paper; it will absorb all the grease, then wash in borax water.

A pinch of salt added to milk will make it more palatable, and more easily digested. A grain of salt added to cream will make it whip more readily.

Doughnuts, cookies, ginger snaps, and crackers stale from long keeping may be freshened by heating through in a moderate oven, and cooling in a dry place.

Parsley may be preserved by taking the green sprigs, washing them and scalding in salt water, then laying on a sieve before the fire to dry as quickly as possible. Put away in a tin box or can it will keep all winter.

Coffee and tea keep best in glass jars.

Doughnuts cut out some time before they are fried and allowed to rise will be much lighter.

If sponge cake is mixed with cold water it will be yellow, if mixed with boiling water it will be white.

To grate a lemon evenly begin at the end and work round it. Nutmegs should be grated at the blossom end.

Celery for Winter use keeps best buried in dry sand, onions spread out on the floor, cabbage packed in a box or cask, stems upward, and covered with leaves.

Apples will keep on shelves in the cellar, or packed in dry sawdust.

To clean brass kettles scour with vinegar and salt.

To make quick vinegar fill a jug with cider, add a little molasses, a liquid yeast, set uncorked near the fire; for two or three days draw off in bottles.

Spices and pepper should be ground fine, put in large mouthed bottles and corked, for use when wanted.

Brown sugar is best for rich puddings and all cooked sweet sauces.

The fishy flavor of wild ducks, if disliked, may be destroyed by scalding the fowls in salt water. Some cooks skin them, as the flavor is in the oil next the skin.

A little borax in the dish water will make glass, china, silver and all tin kitchen utensils clean and bright, and if a pinch is added to the water boiled in the coffee pot twice a week, it will sweeten and purify it.

To chop herbs for seasoning pick the leaves from the stems; if wilted throw them in cold water for a few minutes, then shake free of moisture and chop on a small board with a very sharp knife. Herbs for drying should be gathered in warm, dry weather, picked carefully from the stems, spread on papers and laid in the sun until dry, then packed in paper bags and hung in a dry place.

To clean dried currants for cakes and puddings sprinkle with flour and rub well between the hands, after which turn them into a colander and shake until the stems sift through; put them in a pan, cover with cold water, wash through it and drain, wash again, take from the water, spread on papers or a board and stand in the sun or a cool oven to dry.

To mix mustard use water which has boiled and been allowed to cool; hot water destroys its properties.

To extract the juice of an onion skin a large white onion, grate it on a coarse grater and squeeze in a coarse cloth.

Tough celery unfit for table use may be chopped and put in vinegar for seasoning salads, sauces and soups.

To chop suet for puddings first sprinkle it freely with flour to prevent the pieces adhering.

To keep milk sweet in warm weather add half a teasponful of grated horseradish to a pan of milk.

When eggs are scarce and high use corn starch as a substitute in cakes, puddings and for all thickening purposes. A tablespoonful of corn starch being equal to one egg.

Walnuts which have become dry from long keeping may be freshened by soaking the meats in milk over night. Hickory nuts blanched and pounded are an excellent substitute for almonds in making macaroons and cake fillings.

If cold coffee is kept over for a second serving it should be drained off the grounds, put in a pitcher or stone jar, and added to the fresh coffee in the coffee pot.

The juices of all canned fruits can be used for flavoring and coloring desserts.

Every housekeeper should know that one quart of sifted flour weighs one pound.

Three coffee cups of sifted flour weighs the same.

One pint of soft butter weighs one pound.

One and a half cups of granulated sugar weighs one pound.

Two coffee cups of powdered sugar weighs one pound.

One table spoonful of granulated sugar weighs one ounce.

Ten eggs weighs one pound.

One pint of liquid contains four gills. Four teaspoonsful equal one tablespoon. One wineglass full equals four tablespoons, or two fluid ounces. One common sized tumbler holds half a pint. Four gills make one pint. One large tablespoonful of butter weighs one ounce. One pint of chopped meat weighs one pound. One pint of liquid weighs one pound. Three cups of corn meal weighs one pound.

ELIZA R. PARKER.

www.ingramcontent.com/pod-product-compliance
Lightning Source LLC
Chambersburg PA
CBHW030619270326
41927CB00007B/1245